Recipes by **EMILY LYCOPOLUS**
Photos by **DL ACKEN**

ITALY

RECIPES FOR OLIVE OIL AND VINEGAR LOVERS

TOUCHWOOD EDITIONS

CONTENTS

INTRODUCTION

Like everyone else, I love Italian food. Lucky for me, I married an Italian, and he happens to love Italian food even more than I do! Italian food has so much to offer, and so many options beyond pasta, that cooking Italian food has become a rather wonderful way of life for us. In this book, I share some of our favorite recipes.

Many Italian dishes are quick, simple, and turn out delicious as long as you use quality ingredients. What I've found is that when I use high-quality fused and infused extra virgin olive oils and flavored balsamic vinegars, there's no need to buy and prep an abundance of fresh herbs and spices—all the flavor you need is conveniently and healthfully packed into the bottles.

Unlike dried and even fresh herbs, using infused and fused olive oils ensures that flavor is equally dispersed through the entire dish. Fresh and dried herbs and spices are great, of course, and with time and effort they will give you a similar flavor as the oils—but it won't be as fresh, full, or complete as it would be if you used oil. And it's so much quicker and cleaner to drizzle in some oil than to wash and chop fresh herbs and spices.

And while the health benefits of fresh extra virgin olive oil are incredible, it's the outstanding flavor—the zest, tang, and zip from just one spoonful of high-quality fused or infused olive oil—that keeps people coming back for more.

You don't need to have an entire cupboard of different oils and vinegars to enjoy these dishes. For this book, I've chosen two oils and two vinegars that I use over and over in my Italian cooking. And you'll see that traditional balsamic and extra virgin olive oil—both wonderful pantry staples— also make an appearance. It just seemed wrong to exclude them when they do so much for us! Make sure to always have these on hand.

Of course, if you have a different selection of oils, you can use them in these recipes, too, and get incredible and delicious new results. A pomegranate balsamic is amazing in the Easy Tomato Bruschetta (page 15), for example, so don't be afraid to experiment. These recipes are deliberately versatile and intended to be enjoyed often.

Four simple ingredients—Blood Orange fused olive oil, Tuscan Herb infused olive oil, Fig dark balsamic vinegar, and Sicilian Lemon white balsamic vinegar—can transform everyday food into something exciting and delicious. They make simple recipes taste like you've slaved in the kitchen and your garden all day; no one will guess you whipped up dinner in no time.

I hope you'll enjoy making and eating these recipes as much as my family, my friends, and I do. And I hope they find a place in your home just as they have a place in my home, a place where food can be loved, more time can be spent around the table, and everyone can enjoy being together and eating together.

Fused or infused?

In the olive oil world, the term "fused" is used to refer to olive oil made with the agrumato method; fresh citrus fruit is added to the whole olives, and they are crushed together to extract oil. "Infused" is the term used when herbs or spices are pressed separately and then paired with the olive oil. Both methods ensure the best flavor and standards of food safety. Note that fusing or infusing olive oil should never be done at home. Do your research and always purchase fresh extra virgin olive oil from a reputable source.

TUSCAN HERB INFUSED OLIVE OIL

Take all the fresh herbs that you associate with the Tuscan countryside, and add those flavors together. The **Tuscan Herb infused olive oil** is a complex, earthy, herbaceous delight. It's got all the flavor you could possibly want or need in any savory Italian dish. My husband insists that his eggs are scrambled in this oil. For an incredibly quick and easy, tasty meal, try tossing it with hot pasta and then adding some freshly grated Parmesan cheese for the best butter noodles of your life.

BLOOD ORANGE FUSED OLIVE OIL

The **Blood Orange fused olive oil** is created through the *agrumato* method (see "Fused or infused?" [page 3]). Its flavor is full and fresh, and packs a punch. A little citrus fused olive oil goes a long way, which is why it's my favorite type of oil to use for baking. Not only will your cakes, scones, and muffins be moist while still having the most amazing crumb, their flavor will be delicate yet undeniably present. It's changed the way I bake. No more waiting for butter to come to room temperature and then creaming sugar and butter together for longer than you ever expect it to take—when you use fused oil, you can whip up your recipe much faster, and then your home will be filled with the most intoxicating scent as it bakes!

FIG DARK BALSAMIC VINEGAR

Balsamic vinegar is as classically Italian as you can get in the vinegar world. Fresh, sweet, acidic, and incredibly versatile, this ingredient results in an explosion of flavor when infused. It's like eating the fresh fruit the vinegar has been infused with.

I feature **Fig dark balsamic** in this book, and it can be used in every part of your meal: in your salad dressing and marinades, on ice cream, or as a reduction to accompany a cheese board. Using a single balsamic in this way also ties the flavors of the meal together, which adds a very satisfying note to any occasion.

This vinegar is so rich and delicious. It's very port-like in its flavor profile, so it has a sip-able quality (like an after-dinner digestif). It is the perfect combination of Italian tradition and countryside all poured out of one delicious bottle.

White balsamic is the new kid on the balsamic block. Unlike traditional, caramelized aged balsamic, it is created by reducing crushed grapes in a double boiler-type contraption, which prevents it from caramelizing. It's then aged in stainless steel containers rather than wood so that the vinegar doesn't pick up any color at this stage.

The **Sicilian Lemon white balsamic** that features in this book is tangy and deliciously sweet and tart. It really packs in flavor. This balsamic adds a fresh, acidic punch without too much bite—it can be used in place of lemon juice in many recipes. Play around with some of your favorite recipes to see where you can add it in. The other big advantage of white balsamic is that it has no color. Fresh green salad leaves, chicken, and fish can look a little unappetizing when they're served with a tint of brown, even though the complexity of a dark balsamic might bring out their flavors. This vinegar solves that problem, offering complexity of taste without the color. Add a touch of any white balsamic to milk to make buttermilk, add a tablespoon of it to your eggs and water when you're making pastry for a flaky pie crust that holds its texture, or drop a teaspoonful into sparkling water for a delicious, refreshing drink.

SICILIAN LEMON WHITE BALSAMIC VINEGAR

APPETIZERS

EASY TOMATO BRUSCHETTA

A simple, flexible, appetizer. And here are three ways to serve it: toss it in a bowl and serve it with a spoon alongside other appetizers; spread it on a long Italian loaf, smother with cheese, and bake; or enjoy it with crackers for lunch on a hot summer day when you don't want to turn on the oven. The Tuscan Herb infused olive oil means you don't need to add a lot of extra herbs.

———————————

Crush and roughly chop the garlic, mince the shallot, and then place them both in a medium-sized bowl. Sprinkle with the ½ tsp salt and toss to combine. Chop the tomatoes, rinse well to remove any seeds, pat dry with paper towel or spin gently in a salad spinner, and then add the tomatoes and green onions to the bowl with the garlic and shallot.

Drizzle the olive oil and balsamic over the tomatoes and stir well to combine and coat. Sprinkle with parsley and season to taste with salt and pepper.

You can use this topping immediately, but for the best flavor, allow it to sit for at least 1 hour before dolloping onto the toasted baguette slices and serving.

The topping can be stored in an airtight container in the fridge for up to 1 week.

This is also good with crackers or crostini.

SERVES
FOUR
———
Makes 2 cups

4 garlic cloves

1 shallot

½ tsp flaky sea salt
or kosher salt

6 plum tomatoes

2 green onions

3 Tbsp Tuscan Herb
infused olive oil

1 Tbsp Sicilian Lemon white
balsamic vinegar

2 Tbsp chopped flat-leaf parsley

Sea salt and ground black pepper

1 toasted baguette, sliced

CARPACCIO

Each ingredient in this dish has an important role to play, and they each bring out the best in all the others. Go to a reputable butcher and ask specifically for the best beef sirloin they have. And do let them know you'll be using it for carpaccio. It needs to be sliced paper-thin and used within 2 days of purchase.

———————

Divide the beef slices between two serving plates, placing them in a circle and allowing them to slightly overlap. Drizzle each circle of beef with 1 Tbsp of olive oil and the juice from one lemon wedge. Place ½ cup of arugula in the center of each plate. Sprinkle the Parmesan cheese over top, season to taste with salt and pepper, and serve immediately with a lemon wedge on the side.

SERVES
FOUR

12 paper-thin slices
beef sirloin

2 Tbsp extra virgin olive oil

4 lemon wedges

1 cup arugula

¼ cup shaved Parmesan cheese

Sea salt and ground black pepper

TAPENADE

What makes this tapenade special? Roasting the olives, peppers, and garlic before incorporating them into the other ingredients. This mellows the flavor and adds a lovely smoky-sweet note to the dish. If you love a creamy tapenade, use a blender or food processor. I prefer my tapenade chunky, so I use a mortar and pestle to muddle everything together. Serve alongside Easy Tomato Bruschetta (page 15).

———————————

Preheat the oven to 350°F. Line a baking tray with parchment paper.

Cut the red bell pepper into 1-inch dice, and peel and crush the garlic. Place them on the prepared baking tray. Rinse the olives, pat them dry with a lint-free tea towel or paper towel, and then add them to the baking tray. Drizzle the olive oil over the ingredients and shake the baking tray gently to ensure everything is evenly coated with oil.

Bake for 15 minutes, until the bell pepper and garlic are golden, but not brown. Remove from the oven and allow to cool completely on the baking tray.

Using a large mortar and pestle, gently mash the cooled pepper, garlic, and olives with the capers to combine. Then, using a spoon, mix in the remaining ingredients to fully incorporate. Serve with crostini, crackers, or fresh bread.

This is best enjoyed the day you make it, but can be stored in an airtight container in the fridge for up to 2 days.

1 red bell pepper

4 garlic cloves

2 cups pitted mixed olives

2 Tbsp Tuscan Herb infused olive oil

1 Tbsp capers

2 Tbsp Traditional balsamic vinegar

2 tsp lemon juice

½ tsp sea salt

½ tsp ground black pepper

EASY MARINATED OLIVES
and MOZZARELLA

Use pitted olives for this toss-together appetizer; it allows the flavors to quickly infuse both the inside and outside of the olives, reducing the marinating time. The Tuscan Herb infused olive oil eliminates the need for fresh herbs, which means you can indulge in it all year round.

Place all the ingredients in a small bowl and toss well to combine. Allow to marinate for at least 6 hours before serving, stirring every few hours to ensure the flavors are absorbed evenly.

This can be stored in an airtight container in the fridge for up to 1 week.

SERVES
FOUR
Makes 2 cups

1 cup pitted mixed olives

1 cup cherry-sized balls fresh mozzarella

¼ cup Tuscan Herb infused olive oil

2 Tbsp lemon juice

Sea salt

DEEP-DISH FOCACCIA

There really isn't anything better than the smell of fresh bread, is there? This focaccia is the perfect base for bruschetta (page 15) or tapenade (page 19), or for enjoying with fresh delicious olive oil and balsamic vinegar (Fig dark balsamic is delicious!). I like to make this recipe using Tuscan Herb infused olive oil as it's so herby and delicious, although if I'm feeling like something light and simple, I'll use my favorite robust extra virgin olive oil instead. But no matter what way you enjoy it, it's a guaranteed favorite!

SERVES
FOUR
───
Makes one 9- × 13-inch pan

1½ cups warm (110°F) water

2 Tbsp granulated sugar

2½ tsp active dry yeast

4 cups all-purpose flour, plus extra for kneading

2 Tbsp sea salt, divided

1 cup Tuscan Herb infused olive oil, **divided**

In a large measuring cup, stir together the warm water, sugar, and yeast. Let sit for 10 minutes. The yeast should bubble and foam up if it's alive and happy.

In the bowl of a stand mixer fitted with a paddle attachment, place the flour and 1 Tbsp of the salt. Stir them together, then pour in the yeast mixture and ½ cup of the olive oil. Mix on low speed until the flour is fully incorporated.

Replace the paddle with the dough hook then slowly increase the speed and knead for 5–6 minutes, or until the dough begins to stick to the sides of the bowl and forms a ball. Turn the dough out onto a lightly floured surface and knead for 5 minutes by hand, until it's soft, smooth, and only slightly sticky.

Preheat the oven to 200°F. Turn it off as soon as it comes to temperature.

Pour about 1 tsp of the remaining olive oil into a large mixing bowl, and place the dough in the bowl, turning to coat it evenly with oil. Cover the bowl with a clean, dry tea towel and place it in the warmed oven. Let the dough rise for 1½–2 hours, until it has at least doubled in bulk.

Drizzle a 9- x 13-inch baking dish with 2 Tbsp of the remaining olive oil and use your fingers to spread it evenly across the base and sides of the dish. Place the risen dough in the baking pan and, using your fingertips, gently stretch it into the corners of the pan so it is evenly distributed and fills the pan. Be careful not to tear the dough or press it down too much—the goal is just to stretch it out a little and not to release the gasses from the rising yeast. Cover the dough loosely with a tea towel and let it rest in a warm, draft-free spot for 30–45 minutes.

Preheat the oven to 425°F.

The risen dough should be almost at the top of the baking dish. Using your finger, gently make dimples about 1 inch apart all over the surface of the dough, drizzle it with the remaining olive oil, and sprinkle with the remaining salt.

Place the dish in the oven and turn down the heat to 375°F. Bake for 25 minutes, until golden brown. Remove from the oven and immediately run a knife around the outside of the dish. Allow it to rest for 10 minutes before removing from the baking dish and inviting everyone around you to dive into the delicious warm bread.

This can be stored in an airtight container at room temperature for up to 3 days.

HOMEMADE RICOTTA CHEESE

Making cheese can seem daunting, but this is by far the easiest cheese you can make. And you'll have such a sense of accomplishment at the end. You made cheese! (It tastes even more delicious when you make it yourself.)

The Sicilian Lemon white balsamic provides the perfect balance of acid and sweetness to this super-creamy ricotta. It's perfect to dollop on pizza, spread on crostini drizzled with Fig dark balsamic, or my personal favorite, eaten with honeycomb, roasted Bing cherries, and fresh lemon thyme.

Makes 1½ cups

2 cups whole milk

2 cups heavy (35%) cream

¼ cup Sicilian Lemon white balsamic vinegar

1 tsp sea salt

In a large, heavy-bottomed saucepan, place the milk and cream. Stirring constantly, heat the liquid over medium heat to 190°F. Clipping a candy thermometer to the side of the saucepan is the easiest way to monitor the temperature.

Remove from the heat and add the balsamic and salt. Stir once gently and then let the mixture stand for 10 minutes. Do not be tempted to stir during this time, or you'll change the way the curd forms.

Line a fine strainer with a few layers of cheesecloth, allowing the edges to hang over the sides, and place it over a large bowl. Gently pour the milk mixture (which will now be curds and whey—don't be alarmed by its appearance!) into the cheesecloth and allow to stand for at least 2 hours at room temperature, to allow the curds to fully set and the whey to drain off. You mustn't move it during this time.

Pull up the sides of the cheesecloth to gently squeeze any extra whey into the bowl, leaving only ricotta in the cheesecloth. Discard the whey and transfer the ricotta from the cheesecloth to an airtight container and store it in the fridge for up to 1 week.

CRISPY FRIED POLENTA
and ROASTED CHERRY TOMATOES

Roasted cherry tomatoes are one of my favorite things. Their sweet, slightly salty burst of flavor makes it worth turning on the oven—even in the heat of summer.

2 cups chicken stock

1½ cups yellow cornmeal

½ cup + 4 Tbsp Tuscan Herb infused olive oil

3 cups whole cherry tomatoes

Sea salt and ground black pepper

1 cup ricotta cheese (store-bought or homemade, page 27)

2 Tbsp extra virgin olive oil

Fresh basil for garnish (optional)

Line a 9- × 13-inch baking pan with parchment paper.

In a large, heavy-bottomed saucepan over medium-high heat, heat the chicken stock almost to a boil. Gradually add the cornmeal and cook, stirring occasionally, until soft and creamy and the stock is fully absorbed, 15–20 minutes. Stir in ½ cup infused olive oil, season with salt and pepper. Remove from the heat.

Pour the polenta into the prepared pan and use the back of a spoon to evenly spread it and smooth the top. Place plastic wrap on the surface of the polenta, and place in the fridge for at least 2 hours, or overnight at most.

Preheat the oven to 375°F. Line a baking tray with parchment paper.

Place the cherry tomatoes in a large bowl. Drizzle with 2 Tbsp of infused olive oil and season with salt and pepper. Place on the prepared baking tray, scraping out any last drips of olive oil to drizzle over top. Roast until the tomato skins are bursting and just beginning to brown, 20 minutes. Remove from the oven and let stand for 10 minutes.

In a small bowl, whisk together the ricotta cheese, olive oil, and salt and pepper until everything is fully incorporated and the ricotta is creamy and fluffy. Place in the fridge, uncovered, to set for 15 minutes, or up to overnight.

When ready to serve, heat a frying pan over medium heat and pour in the remaining 2 Tbsp of Tuscan Herb infused olive oil. Cut the polenta into triangles and fry until golden brown, 1–2 minutes per side. Serve the fried polenta topped with cherry tomatoes and a dollop of ricotta. Garnish with fresh basil, if desired.

HOW TO BUILD THE

PERFECT
CHARCUTERIE
&
CHEESE
BOARD

When executed well, a charcuterie and cheese board is a thing of beauty. The secret to its success lies in the skilful pairing of complementary flavors, colors, and textures. Make room for items sweet and savory, hard and soft, crunchy and smooth.

MEAT & CHEESE

I always start by choosing the meat and cheese, typically three types of each. As a general rule, you can expect each person to eat 2 ounces of meat and 2 ounces of cheese. If I'm making a board for four people, I err on the side of generous and will buy 2–3 ounces of each type of meat and cheese. It also depends on how long the event is likely to last. For a cocktail party or a gourmet movie night, which will last around 3 hours, I'll allow for 3 ounces per person. For a pre-dinner snack or savory dessert, 2 ounces per person should be fine. Having said that, who ever complains about having leftover cheese in the fridge?

When choosing the meats, try to mix it up. For example, feature a cured sausage-style meat (salami, for example), a cured sliced meat (like prosciutto), and a pâté (duck rillettes is always scrumptious, but a good-quality chicken liver pâté also makes a delicious addition and is usually easier to find in North America).

For the cheese, the rule of thumb is to choose a hard cheese (like Parmesan or aged Asiago), something soft (goat cheese or a younger Cheddar, for example), and a rind-ripened cheese (Brie or Camembert are always a hit). If I know that blue cheese lovers will be joining the mix, I always add some crumbled Gorgonzola. Danish blue is also a lovely addition for color, flavor, and texture (for everything, really!). I also look for variety in shape among the cheeses to ensure the board has esthetic appeal. A wedge or a slice, plus a round or wheel of a cheese set beside a crumbled cheese or rectangle make the board appealing to the eye.

EXTRAS

Once I've decided on the meats and cheeses, I start
to think about the extras (the accessories, if you like). I
always include honey (wildflower honey is my favorite to
pair with strong aged cheese as it's neutral and not sickly
sweet; clover honey comes a close second; and if you're
feeling really adventurous, try a lavender flower honey)
to pair with the hard aged cheese, a balsamic reduction
to pair with the ripened cheese, some olive oil, of course
(medium robust is best—you don't want anything either too
strong that will totally overpower the milder cheeses or that
will just disappear—such as a rich Nocellara del Belice,
mild Leccino, or Coratina), and nuts, olives, and fruit (fresh
or dried) to nibble on. Walnuts and toasted almonds both
pair beautifully with any blue cheese; apples and pears
are perfect to enjoy alongside Brie; figs and cherries pair
well with prosciutto; and grainy mustard will add that
special something to any salami selection. Lay out some
grissini, fresh bread, and crackers to use as vehicles to
enjoy everything with, add in some beautiful spoons and
little dishes, and you're set!

CHEESE

Blue
Gorgonzola

Soft
Fontina

Fresh mozzarella or Bocconcini

Goat

Italian goat/ Caprino Fresco

Marscapone

Ricotta

Young Cheddar

Rind-ripened
Brie

Camembert

Robiola

Taleggio

Hard
Aged Asiago

Aged Piave

Parmesan

Pecorino Romano

Ricotto Salata

MEAT

Pâté
Chicken liver pâté

Sausage-style
Genoa salami

Hot and mild Calabrese salami

Pepperoni

Sopressata

Sliced & cured
Bresaola

Capicollo

Coppa

Guanciale

Mortadella

Pancetta

Prosciutto

NUTS & FRUIT

Toasted almonds or walnuts, pistachios

Dried apricots, cherries, cranberries, or figs

Fresh apple or pear slices

BREAD & CRACKERS

Baguette

Crusty sourdough

Focaccia

Grissini

Rice crackers

Whole grain/seedy crisps

CONDIMENTS

Balsamic reduction (see page 32)

Honey (wildflower, clover, lavender)

Robust extra-virgin olive oil (like Nocellara del Belice, mild Leccino, or Coratina)

Sweet or savory chutney

Whole grain mustard

Antipasto or tapenade

Marinated olives

Roasted red peppers

SOUPS

&

SALADS

PANZANELLA SALAD

Would you like some salad with your croutons? I like to use fresh bread for this, as it soaks up the oil and vinegar better than day-old bread. Make sure you add the croutons right at the end so that they don't absorb too much moisture from the other ingredients.

SERVES
TWO

4 cups 1-inch cubes of bread

½ Spanish or red onion, roughly chopped

½ cup + 2 Tbsp Tuscan Herb infused olive oil

2 Tbsp Sicilian Lemon white balsamic vinegar

Sea salt and ground black pepper

2 cup whole cherry tomatoes

1 cup pitted mixed olives

1 Tbsp Fig dark balsamic vinegar

1 tsp Dijon mustard

1 tsp honey

Preheat the oven to 325°F. Line a baking tray with parchment paper.

Place the bread cubes and onion in a bowl. Drizzle with ½ cup of the olive oil and the Sicilian Lemon balsamic and toss to ensure everything is well coated. Spread them onto the prepared baking tray and sprinkle with salt and pepper to taste.

Bake the bread and onion for 10 minutes, and then remove the baking tray from the oven. Using a spatula, turn the croutons over and bake for an additional 5 minutes, until they're golden brown and the onion is slightly roasted (its edges should be curling a little and just turning brown).

Remove from the oven and allow to cool on the baking tray.

Meanwhile, halve the cherry tomatoes and roughly chop the olives, and divide them evenly between two serving bowls.

In a small mixing bowl, whisk together the 2 Tbsp olive oil, the Fig balsamic, mustard, and honey. Drizzle this dressing evenly over the tomatoes and olives. Toss to combine.

Divide the onion evenly between the bowls and toss gently to combine. Finally, divide the croutons between the bowls and toss gently to combine. The dressing will be very light—you don't want the bread to be soggy. Enjoy immediately.

SHAVED FENNEL SALAD
with BLOOD ORANGES

...tra-simple salad is the perfect way to enjoy blood ... In winter, this salad reminds me of summer. In ...hen blood oranges aren't in season, I often make ...pink grapefruit or Cara Cara oranges instead. ...ood Orange fused olive oil and Sicilian Lemon white balsamic create a lovely citrus blend.

In a serving bowl, whisk together the olive oil, balsamic, mustard, and honey until emulsified.

Using a mandoline, shave the fennel bulb and shallot into paper-thin strips. Toss them into the dressing and use your hands to gently coat them evenly.

Segment the blood oranges and arrange the segments on top of the fennel.

Now chiffonade the mint: stack the mint leaves together so they're all facing the same direction, and then gently but firmly roll the leaves lengthwise to form a small tube. Using a sharp knife, cut across the mint tube to create tiny ribbons of mint. Gently separate and fluff the mint with your fingers and sprinkle it over top the salad, if desired.

This is best served immediately, although it will keep in an airtight container in the fridge for 1 day.

SERVES
TWO
for lunch or 4 as a side

¼ cup Blood Orange fused olive oil

1 Tbsp Sicilian Lemon white balsamic vinegar

1 Tbsp grainy Dijon mustard

1 Tbsp honey

1 large fennel bulb

1 shallot

2 blood oranges

2-3 sprigs mint

LEMON GRILLED CAESAR SALAD

This is the perfect side dish for summer barbecue evenings when you want to host a very low-maintenance dinner. We serve this with grilled steak or chicken, roasted or grilled seasonal vegetables, and ice cream for dessert. Simple and delicious, it also leaves you with lots of time to catch up with your guests. If it's not summer or a grill isn't handy, this salad also tastes great without the grill marks.

SERVES
FOUR

2 garlic cloves

¼ tsp sea salt

½ cup + 2 Tbsp extra virgin olive oil

2 Tbsp Sicilian Lemon white balsamic vinegar

1 Tbsp lemon juice

1 tsp Worcestershire sauce

¼ cup mayonnaise

2 hearts of romaine

1 cup lardons or bacon bits

½ cup shaved Parmesan cheese

2 Tbsp capers

1 tsp lemon zest

Using the back of a knife, crush the garlic cloves and then roughly chop them. Using a mortar and pestle, mash the garlic with the sea salt to form a paste. Add the ½ cup of olive oil, the balsamic, lemon juice, and Worcestershire sauce, and whisk to fully combine. Add the mayo and whisk again until smooth and creamy. Set aside.

On a large cutting board, halve the hearts of romaine lengthwise. Gently rinse and pat each half dry and brush the cut sides with the 2 Tbsp olive oil.

Preheat a barbecue grill or frying pan to medium heat. Place the lettuce cut-side down on the grill and grill for 1 minute, until the leaves are just beginning to brown and grill marks are visible.

Divide the lettuce evenly between four plates. Drizzle each plate of lettuce with 2–3 Tbsp of dressing. Top with bacon bits, Parmesan cheese, and capers. Drizzle an additional tablespoon of dressing over top each plated salad, and finish with a scattering of lemon zest.

Serve immediately. (I find a steak knife is the best way to cut up the lettuce.)

EVERYDAY GREEN SALAD

My Aunt Maria had a theory: a good salad must be hand-tossed! Even when she was making a banquet dinner for 500-plus people, she would be up to her armpits in lettuce, tossing it by hand. This is a simple, delicious salad she would make for every meal.

———————

Wash the lettuce in cold water and pat dry with a clean tea towel (or use a salad spinner if you have one—I don't!). Tear the lettuce leaves from the stem and place them in a serving bowl. Drizzle with the olive oil and balsamic and sprinkle with salt to taste.

Wash and dry your hands well, and toss the lettuce in the oil and vinegar, massaging the leaves so they are all evenly coated.

This is perfect with either lunch or dinner. (Or even as lunch itself!)

SERVES
TWO-FOUR
———

1 head of lettuce (Boston, leaf, romaine, or a combination)

2 Tbsp extra virgin olive oil

2 Tbsp Sicilian Lemon White balsamic vinegar

Sea salt

SPRING FARRO SALAD

For me, the best part of this salad is the dressing. Tossing it with the farro while it's still warm allows the farro to soak up all the flavor and prevents the salad from becoming soggy, which makes it just that little bit different from lots of other salads. And did I mention that it tastes amazing?

───────────────

In a large saucepan, cover the farro with 3 cups of water, add a sprinkle of salt, and bring to a boil over medium heat. Turn down the heat to low and simmer, uncovered, for 20 minutes, until the farro is al dente.

Drain the farro and put it into a large bowl. Immediately drizzle the olive oil and balsamic over top the warm farro and mix to combine. Set aside, uncovered, to cool completely at room temperature.

Slice the bell pepper into long, thin strips, peel and segment the grapefruit, and wash the spring greens. Add them to the cool farro and toss to combine.

Divide the farro evenly between four plates. Peel and slice the avocado. Top the salads with slices of avocado and 2 Tbsp of feta cheese.

You can make the farro and toss it with the dressing up to a day ahead of time, but don't add the other ingredients until you're ready to eat.

SERVES
FOUR
───

2 cups farro

Sea salt and ground black pepper

¼ cup Blood Orange
fused olive oil

¼ cup Fig dark balsamic vinegar

1 red bell pepper

1 ruby grapefruit

3 cups spring greens (try a mix
of arugula, baby kale, mustard
greens, pea shoots, etc.)

1 avocado

½ cup crumbled feta cheese

NANA'S CHICKEN SOUP

There's something special about homemade chicken soup—especially this one, although technically it's a broth rather than a soup. It's the only thing I crave if I feel a cold coming on, and nothing can beat it on a miserable winter day. I also use it in summer as the base for many dishes, and always keep a few tubs of it in the freezer. This is the chicken broth that I use in the Passatelli, Minestrone, and Italian Wedding soups (pages 51-55).

Makes about 8 quarts

1 whole stewing hen (small chicken)

1 yellow onion

2 carrots

2 stalks celery

1 tomato

2 Tbsp Tuscan Herb infused olive oil

———

Place the stewing hen in a large (8–12 quart) stockpot and fill the pot with water to within 3 inches of the top.

Peel the onion, but leave it whole. Pierce it a few times with a paring knife and then add it to the pot. Wash the carrots and celery and then chop them in half. Pierce the tomato and add all the veggies and olive oil to the pot. Cover with a lid and bring to a rolling boil over high heat. As soon as it's boiling, turn down the heat to the lowest setting and cook, covered, for 6–8 hours, until the chicken is cooked through.

Remove chicken carcass from the broth, and then strain the broth by scooping out vegetables with a slotted spoon or mesh sieve.

Allow the broth to cool to room temperature, about 1 hour, then place it in the fridge, uncovered, to chill.

Remove the meat from the chicken and reserve it to add to the broth (or to use in chicken salad sandwiches). You can discard the vegetables, although they're great to snack on or use as dog treats.

Reheat the broth as needed. It keeps well in an airtight container in the fridge for up to 1 week, or in large freezer bags or containers in the freezer for up to 6 months.

PASSATELLI

This soup features a unique kind of pasta—it's made from bread crumbs, eggs, Parmesan, and parsley, and then pressed through a meat grinder or ricer. When my husband was a boy, he called this worm soup—and, unfortunately, it does look very much like worms having a swim. Fortunately, it tastes much better than it looks.

SERVES
FOUR

2 cups dried bread crumbs

1¼ cups grated Parmesan cheese, divided

1 cup grated Romano cheese

2 Tbsp dried parsley

4 eggs

¼ cup Tuscan Herb infused olive oil

1 tsp sea salt

½ tsp ground black pepper

½ tsp ground nutmeg

8 cups chicken broth (page 49)

Line a baking sheet with parchment paper and dust it with flour. Set aside.

In a large mixing bowl, combine the bread crumbs, 1 cup of the Parmesan, the Romano, and parsley with the eggs, olive oil, salt, pepper, and nutmeg, mixing well to form a thick paste. Form the mixture into a ball, wrap it tightly in plastic, and let it rest for 2 hours in the fridge.

Using a meat grinder or a potato ricer with a fitting for larger holes, take small sections of the dough and press it through, making little round tubes (the passatelli).

Using a sharp knife, cut the passatelli from the base of the ricer once they're 4–5 inches long and lay them on the prepared baking sheet. Dust them with a little bit of flour to prevent them from sticking.

To make the soup, heat the broth in a large saucepan over medium-high heat to almost a boil. Carefully add the passatelli and cook for 5–6 minutes, until the passatelli have swollen a little and are soft and cooked through.

Garnish with a dusting of the remaining Parmesan cheese and serve with fresh focaccia (page 22).

Uncooked passatelli can be frozen for up to 3 months. Freeze them on a baking tray and then transfer them to freezer bags. Cooked passatelli will keep in the broth in an airtight container in the fridge for up to 1 day.

MINESTRONE SOUP

This hearty soup is lovely on a cold day. Bursting with rich flavors and a variety of textures, it offers every kind of tasty goodness you could desire—no wonder it's always a hit.

SERVES
FOUR

Chop the onion and mince the garlic. In a large saucepan, sauté them in the olive oil over medium heat until just translucent.

While the onion and garlic are cooking, chop the celery into ½-inch pieces and peel and roughly chop the carrots. Add them to the saucepan. Sprinkle in the salt, to allow the onion to sweat, and sauté for another 3–4 minutes, until the onion is golden and the celery and carrots are starting to soften. Pour in the juice from the tomatoes, then add the tomatoes, gently crushing them in your hand first. Pour in the chicken broth and bring the soup to a boil over medium-high heat, cover, turn down the heat to low, and simmer for 25 minutes. Remove the lid, bring the soup back to a boil over high heat, and add the beans and pasta. Cook until the pasta is al dente, about 10 minutes. Serve immediately with crusty bread.

This soup can be refrigerated in an airtight container for a couple of days. It can also be frozen for up to 3 months without the pasta.

1 yellow onion

2 cloves garlic

¼ cup Tuscan Herb infused olive oil

2 stalks celery

2 carrots

1 tsp sea salt

1 (28 oz) can whole tomatoes

3 cups chicken broth (page 49)

1 (19 oz) can kidney beans, rinsed and drained

1 cup dried fusilli pasta

Fresh flat-leaf parsley and basil

ITALIAN WEDDING SOUP

I love this soup when I'm looking for a light dinner on a cool evening. Serve it with crusty Italian bread or Deep-Dish Focaccia (page 22) and Everyday Green Salad (page 45). Blissful simplicity.

———————————

In a mixing bowl, toss the ground beef, pork, eggs, olive oil, minced garlic, grated onion, bread crumbs, Parmesan, parsley, and salt together and mix thoroughly. I use my hands for this, kneading everything until fully combined.

Using about 1 Tbsp of the meat mixture per meatball, form small balls (they'll be about 1 inch in diameter) and set them on a baking tray. (At this point, you can freeze the meatballs on the baking tray and then transfer them to freezer bags to have on hand so you can make this soup in a flash. Just be sure to let them thaw before using.)

In a large stockpot over medium-high heat, bring the chicken broth to a boil, uncovered. Add the meatballs and cook for 5 minutes, then add the spinach and orzo and cook until the pasta is al dente and the meatballs are cooked through, 5–8 minutes. Ladle into serving bowls and top with Parmesan cheese.

This will keep in an airtight container in the fridge for a couple of days. If you want to freeze it, freeze the broth and meatballs separately.

SERVES
FOUR
———

1 cup ground beef

1 cup ground pork

2 eggs

2 Tbsp Tuscan Herb infused olive oil

2 cloves garlic, minced

½ small red onion, grated

1 cup dried bread crumbs

½ cup grated Parmesan cheese

2 tsp dried parsley

1 tsp salt

8 cups chicken broth (page 49)

4 cups torn baby spinach leaves

2 cups orzo pasta

¼ cup grated or shaved Parmesan cheese, for serving

PIZZA

PERFECT PIZZA DOUGH

When it comes to pizza, I like to keep it easy. This dough is ready in about 25 minutes, which is usually about the amount of time it takes to get the toppings chopped and the sauce ready. The trick to making really good pizza is a really hot oven! Preheat your oven to as hot as it can go and keep the door closed while it heats to get the temperature hot (and I mean *hot!*).

Makes one 12-14" pizza

4 cups all-purpose flour

2 Tbsp granulated sugar

1 Tbsp quick-rising yeast

½ tsp baking soda

1 tsp sea salt

1½ cups very hot (115°F) water

½ cup + 1½ tsp extra virgin olive oil (or try Tuscan Herb infused olive oil!)

In a large bowl, whisk 3 cups of the flour with the sugar, yeast, soda, and salt until fully combined and the flour is slightly fluffy. Transfer the dry ingredients to a stand mixer fitted with the dough hook attachment.

Add the water and ½ cup olive oil to the flour mixture. Mix until fully combined and then continue to knead the dough for 10 minutes, slowly adding the remaining cup of flour ¼ cup at a time while the machine is running to prevent the dough from sticking. (At this point the dough can be put in the fridge to rise overnight or placed in the freezer and frozen for up to 3 months. Frozen dough should be left to thaw to room temperature then allowed to rise, covered and set in a warm place, as directed.)

Drizzle the 1½ tsp of olive oil into a bowl, and add the dough, turning it once to coat with oil. Cover the bowl with a clean, dry tea towel and let the dough rise for 10 minutes in a warm, draft-free spot. I love to set it on the back of the stovetop while the oven is preheating.

To bake the dough into pizza, preheat the oven to 450°F (or as high as your oven will go).

Once the dough has doubled in bulk, remove it from the bowl and place it on a pizza stone or baking tray. Stretch out the dough to cover the pan, being careful not to tear it. Top with your desired toppings, using the recipes on pages 62–65 as inspiration.

EASY PIZZA SAUCE

I use regular canned tomato juice for this. (Leftovers are great in a Bloody Mary.) This is one of the few recipes where garlic is added to liquid ingredients without being sautéed first. Doing it this way allows it to dissolve right into the sauce. This recipe makes ¾ cup, which is enough for one pizza, but I like to double or triple it, and keep it in portioned containers in the freezer for convenience.

———————————

In a small saucepan, bring the tomato juice, garlic, olive oil, balsamic, parsley, and oregano to boil over medium-high heat and reduce to about half, 20–30 minutes.

Whisk in the tomato paste and remove from the heat. Allow to cool slightly before using.

Makes ¾ cup

1 cup tomato juice

2 cloves garlic, crushed

1 Tbsp Tuscan Herb infused
olive oil

1 tsp Traditional balsamic vinegar

1 tsp dried parsley

½ tsp dried oregano

2 Tbsp tomato paste

FRESH FIG, PROSCIUTTO, and ARUGULA PIZZA

Preheat the oven to 475°F.

Prepare the pizza dough. Spread the sauce over top. Top with 1½ cups of the cheese. Arrange the figs evenly on the dough. Cut the prosciutto into 2-inch strips and place them evenly over the pizza. Sprinkle the remaining cheese over top.

Bake for 10–15 minutes, until the prosciutto is crisp, the figs are roasted, the cheese is bubbly, and the crust is golden. Remove from the oven, top with the arugula, and drizzle with the balsamic. Serve immediately.

Makes one 12-14" pizza

1 recipe Perfect Pizza Dough

¾ cup Easy Pizza Sauce

2 cups grated mozzarella cheese

4-5 fresh figs, cut into ½-inch-thick slices

6 strips of prosciutto

2 cups arugula

1 Tbsp Fig dark balsamic vinegar

MARGHERITA PIZZA

Preheat the oven to 475°F.

Prepare the pizza dough. Spread the sauce over top. Drizzle the olive oil over the sauce and then sprinkle with the grated mozzarella. Slice the buffalo mozzarella into ½-inch-thick slices. Arrange the slices evenly over the pizza and top with basil leaves.

Bake for 8–10 minutes, until the cheese is bubbly and the crust is golden brown.

Makes one 12-14" pizza

1 recipe Perfect Pizza Dough

¾ cup Easy Pizza Sauce

1 tsp Tuscan Herb infused olive oil

1 cup grated mozzarella cheese

1 large buffalo mozzarella cheese ball

½ cup fresh basil leaves

ROASTED FENNEL, ITALIAN SAUSAGE, and YELLOW TOMATO PIZZA

Preheat the oven to 475°F.

Prepare the pizza dough. Spread the sauce over top. Sprinkle with half the cheese and set aside.

Take the outer layers of the fennel off the bulb and shave them with a mandoline. Discard the inner leaves. Spread half the shaved fennel over the pizza crust.

Squeeze the Italian sausages from their casings into a small frying pan over medium heat. Using a wooden spoon, separate and fry the sausage flesh until it's slightly brown. Drain off the fat and sprinkle the sausage over the pizza. Sprinkle the remaining cheese over the pizza, top with the remaining shaved fennel and slices of yellow tomato, and drizzle with the olive oil.

Bake for 10–15 minutes, until the fennel is roasted, the cheese is bubbly, and the crust is golden. Serve immediately.

Makes one 12-14" pizza

1 recipe Perfect Pizza Dough

¾ cup Easy Pizza Sauce

2 cups grated mozzarella cheese

1 fennel bulb

2 fresh Italian sausages

1 large yellow tomato

2 Tbsp Tuscan Herb infused olive oil

WHITE PIZZA with SPINACH and RICOTTA

Preheat the oven to 475°F.

Drizzle the prepared pizza dough generously with the olive oil and use the back of a spoon to spread it all over the crust, right to the edges. Using a mortar and pestle, or the back of a knife, mash the garlic with the salt to form a paste. Spread this over the crust and sprinkle with the Parmesan cheese.

Place the dough in the oven for 6 minutes to par-bake the crust. This ensures the white pizza won't get soggy. As soon as you remove it from the oven, sprinkle with 1 cup of the mozzarella cheese.

Using a mandoline or very sharp knife, thinly slice the shallot and evenly distribute the shavings over the pizza. Top with the spinach and then the ricotta, dropping it in generous spoonfuls over the pizza. Sprinkle with the remaining mozzarella and the pinch of chili flakes.

Bake for 10–15 minutes, until the ricotta has puffed up, the mozzarella is golden and bubbly, and the crust is golden too. Serve immediately.

Makes one 12-14" pizza

1 recipe Perfect Pizza Dough

2 Tbsp Tuscan Herb infused olive oil

2 garlic cloves

½ tsp sea salt

2 Tbsp freshly grated Parmesan cheese

2 cups grated mozzarella cheese, divided

1 shallot

2 cups baby spinach leaves

1 cup ricotta cheese (store-bought or homemade, page 27)

Pinch of chili flakes

PASTA

FRESH PASTA

Fresh pasta is delightful. There's no comparing it to the dried versions you buy at the store. The texture of fresh pasta also grabs sauce better than dried pasta does. Fresh tagliatelle (pictured on page 72) is much softer and suppler than the dried version, so I find it works best with creamy, smooth sauces like Alfredo or rosé. Master a couple of the sauce recipes on pages 75–79, and you'll never be caught out by unexpected visitors again! Different pasta shapes work best with different sauces, so check the recommended pasta shape below each recipe. I've also given you two fun variations if you're looking for a bit of color.

SERVES

TWO

4 eggs

5 Tbsp extra virgin olive oil

2 cups all-purpose flour, plus extra for dusting

½ tsp sea salt

In a mixing bowl, whisk two of the eggs with 2 Tbsp of the olive oil, and then whisk in the remaining two eggs and 2 Tbsp of the remaining olive oil. Gently whisk in 1 cup of the flour and the salt to form a yellow, creamy paste. Swap your whisk for a wooden spoon to stir and sprinkle in just enough of the remaining 1 cup of flour to allow the dough to pull away from the sides of the bowl. Sprinkle the remaining flour on the counter, turn the dough out onto it, and knead until all the flour has been absorbed and the dough is very smooth and elastic. Divide the dough into four pieces and form them into small balls. Drizzle them with a little of the remaining 1 Tbsp of olive oil to prevent a skin from forming. Let rest, uncovered, on the kitchen counter for 10 minutes.

Using a rolling pin (or pasta maker), roll out one ball of dough at a time, dusting both sides with some additional flour to prevent it from drying. (This might seem counterintuitive, but the flour keeps the dough soft and supple, and easy to work with.) Run the pasta sheets through a pasta maker (or roll out thinly with a rolling pin and then cut with a sharp knife or pizza cutter) to form the desired shape and size.

To cook fresh pasta, bring a saucepan of heavily salted water to a rolling boil over high heat with a little bit of the remaining olive oil. Add the pasta, and stir to ensure it doesn't stick. Turn down the heat to medium-high and cook for 2–3 minutes, until cooked through and soft. Add to the sauce of your choice as soon as it's cooked.

To make tomato pasta:

Whisk 2 Tbsp of tomato paste with the olive oil before you add the flour. Increase the flour by ½ cup.

To make spinach pasta:

Using a blender, blend the eggs with ½ cup fresh spinach until the spinach is puréed and smooth before adding the eggs to the recipe as directed above. Increase the flour by ½ cup.

SIMPLE POMODORO SAUCE

A simple tomato sauce is one of the best examples of a recipe where *meh* ingredients will result in a finished product that is edible but not amazing. Use the freshest, best quality, most amazing ingredients you can lay your hands on and you'll have a finished product that is truly swoon-inducing. If you don't have fresh tomatoes and a food mill, use the best canned Roma tomatoes available instead.

———————————

Slice the tomatoes in half and, using a food mill, crush them into a large saucepan. (If using canned tomatoes, carefully pour in the juice and then gently crush the tomatoes in your hand before adding them to the pot.) Turn on the heat to medium and bring to a simmer, stirring frequently to prevent the tomatoes from sticking. Once the tomatoes start to bubble, turn down the heat to medium-low.

Using the back of a knife, crush the garlic, remove the center stem from each clove, and add the crushed cloves to the tomatoes.

Finely mince the shallot. In a small saucepan, warm the oil over medium heat and then add the shallot. Cook until it's just soft and turning brown, about 3 minutes.

Add the oil and shallot to the tomato sauce. Sprinkle in the sugar, half the basil, and salt and pepper to taste. Continue to cook over medium heat, stirring occasionally, until the sauce is thick and the basil has wilted, 2–3 minutes.

Add the remaining basil just before serving with pasta; or transfer the sauce to an airtight container, lay some basil on top, and allow to cool before storing in the fridge for up to 1 week.

Makes about 3 cups
Best served with bucatini,
spaghetti, tagliatelle

8 Roma tomatoes
(or use a 28 oz can)

4 cloves garlic

1 shallot

2 Tbsp extra virgin olive oil

1 Tbsp granulated sugar

½ cup freshly torn basil, divided

Sea salt and ground black pepper

ALFREDO-STYLE SAUCE

Alfredo is delicious and easy to make, but preparing it requires your undivided attention, which makes multitasking a challenge. So, for me, Alfredo is either a special occasion sauce or something I make when I have an unbearable craving for it. I use this recipe in Baked Cheese Ravioli (page 86), but it's also amazing when served with fresh tomato pasta (page 71) and a drizzle of exquisite olive oil. There are many variations on this classic favorite, but I like mine extra-creamy.

In a large saucepan, heat the milk and cream to a simmer over medium heat. Do not let them come to a boil.

In a separate saucepan—or in a frying pan—heat the oil over medium heat and then add the flour. Using a small whisk, combine the flour with the oil. The flour will start to bubble. Continue whisking until a paste is formed and the bubbling has almost stopped, about 2 minutes. Slowly ladle in the warm cream-milk mixture, about ½ cup at a time, whisking as you add each batch. The sauce will gradually start to thicken. Once all the cream-milk mixture has been added and the sauce is thick, remove from the heat. Whisk in the garlic and nutmeg and then whisk in half of the chopped parsley. Gradually add the cheeses, about ½ cup at a time, whisking well after each addition. Season to taste with salt and pepper.

Use the remaining parsley to garnish the finished pasta dish. This sauce is best used as soon as it's cooked.

Makes 2½ cups
Best served with farfalle,
fettucine, tagliatelle

1 cup whole milk

1 cup whipping (35%) cream

¼ cup Tuscan Herb infused olive oil

¼ cup all-purpose flour

3 cloves garlic, crushed

Pinch of ground nutmeg

2 Tbsp chopped flat-leaf parsley, divided

1 cup grated Parmesan cheese

½ cup grated mozzarella cheese

Sea salt and ground black pepper

BOLOGNESE (MEAT) SAUCE

This traditional Italian meat sauce is ideal. Try it in place of the mushrooms for a carnivore-friendly version of my Creamy Polenta with Roasted Mushrooms and Shaved Parmesan (page 97).

———————————

Finely chop the onion and mince the garlic. In a large saucepan, over medium heat, sauté the onion and garlic in the olive oil until the onion is just translucent, about 2 minutes. Add the ground beef and pork, and continue cooking until the meat is almost fully browned, the onion is soft, and the garlic is golden. Drain off any extra juices, reserving ½ cup.

Carefully pour the tomato juice from the can into the saucepan, keeping all the tomatoes in the can. Stirring constantly and keeping the heat at medium, simmer the juice with the meat mixture. Do not let it come to a boil. You don't want any evaporation.

Using a blender or food mill, crush/pulse the canned tomatoes until they form a smooth purée. (If you prefer some chunks, as I sometimes do, hold each tomato over the pan and crush it in your hand instead of blending.) Add this purée to the meat mixture and continue to cook, stirring constantly, for about 5 minutes. Add the herbs and allow the sauce to reduce over medium-low heat for at least 10 minutes, until you have your ideal texture (sometimes I let it reduce for 20 minutes). Add the tomato paste and stir to fully incorporate. Cook for an additional 2 minutes and then remove from the heat. Serve with a garnish of grated Parmesan cheese and salt and pepper to taste.

You can store this in an airtight container in the fridge for up to 1 week or in the freezer for up to 3 months.

Makes 6 generous cups
Best served with cavatelli,
conchiglie, pappardelle, penne—
and perfect in lasagna, of course.

This recipe is as tasty to eat
as it is messy to prepare.
I recommend wearing an
apron when cooking this!

1 large yellow onion

4 cloves garlic

2 Tbsp Tuscan Herb infused olive oil

1 lb extra-lean ground beef

1 lb lean ground pork

1 (28 oz) can Roma tomatoes

2 sprigs rosemary

4 sprigs thyme

¼ cup flat-leaf parsley

¼ cup fresh basil leaves

1 (5½ oz) can tomato paste

Grated Parmesan cheese for garnish

Sea salt and ground black pepper

HOMEMADE GREMOLATA
(PARSLEY LEMON PESTO)

This unique pesto is native to the north of Italy and is a lovely contrast to most basil-based pestos. It's also nut-free, which makes it a delicious treat for anyone with nut allergies. Serve this with ricotta on crostini for an appetizer, toss it with fresh pasta, or use it like an Italian-style chimichurri sauce on chicken or steak.

———————

Place all the ingredients in a blender or food processor in the order listed and blend into a smooth paste.

Store this in an airtight container in the fridge for up to 1 week or in ice trays in the freezer for up to 3 months.

Makes 1½ cups
Best served with farfalle, fusilli, spaghetti

¼ cup extra virgin olive oil

2 Tbsp Sicilian Lemon white balsamic vinegar

2 large bunches flat-leaf parsley

6 cloves garlic

¼ cup mint leaves

1 Tbsp lemon zest

ORECCHIETTE CARBONARA
with SPRING PEAS and PANCETTA

This dish perfectly combines the fresh, light taste of spring with the richness of cozy, comfort food. If pancetta isn't available, thick-cut bacon strips cut into ½-inch pieces before frying turns out just as well.

———————————

In a small frying pan, fry the pancetta until just crisp. Place the fried slices on paper towel to absorb any excess grease.

Using a mortar and pestle, smash the garlic clove with a little salt to form a paste and then whisk in the olive oil.

In a saucepan, whisk the egg with the yolks. Add the olive oil-garlic mixture and place over low heat. Whisk until creamy and thick, 5–8 minutes. (You can also do this in a double boiler, if you prefer. It will take 10–12 minutes to thicken.) Whisk in the ½ cup Parmesan cheese and continue whisking over low heat until the sauce is thick and velvety smooth.

Cook the orecchiette in a large saucepan of heavily salted, boiling water, stirring to ensure it doesn't stick. Drain the pasta and add it to the sauce, mixing well to coat. Serve with peas, the pancetta slices, and some Parmesan for garnish. Enjoy immediately.

SERVES
TWO
———

6 oz sliced pancetta

1 clove garlic

Sea salt

2 Tbsp Tuscan Herb infused olive oil

1 egg

2 egg yolks

½ cup grated Parmesan cheese, plus extra for garnish

½ cup blanched fresh green peas or thawed frozen green peas

2½ cups dried orecchiette

LASAGNA

This is my husband's favorite meal. It's delicious but fussy to make, so I typically make several at a time and then freeze them. Later, I bake the thawed-out lasagnas in a water bath, as described on page 83.

———————————

Grease a 7- x 11-inch lasagna or baking dish (or two loaf pans) with a little bit of olive oil. Set aside. Bring a large saucepan of heavily salted water to a boil over high heat.

Cut the sheets of fresh pasta to the length of your baking dish and then place them in the boiling water for 2–3 minutes to par-boil. Remove them from the water and drain. Drizzle with a bit of olive oil to prevent them from sticking and stack them on a cutting board until you're ready to cook them.

In a mixing bowl, whisk together the ricotta cheese, eggs, and olive oil.

To assemble the lasagna, place a thin layer of meat sauce on the bottom of the dish. Top with a single layer of the pasta, allowing the pasta sheets to touch but not overlap too much. Pour a thin layer of meat sauce over the pasta, then drizzle with one-third of the ricotta mixture and gently spread it evenly over top the meat sauce.

Sprinkle 1 cup of the mozzarella over top. Repeat these layers—pasta–meat sauce–ricotta–mozzarella—twice, so you have three layers of pasta and end with mozzarella.

Place in the fridge to set, at least 1 hour or up to overnight, or freeze as is for up to 6 months.

When you're ready to eat, preheat the oven to 350°F and bake the lasagna for 45 minutes until it's cooked through, bubbling, and hot, and the cheese is golden on top.

Allow the lasagna to cool for 10 minutes before slicing. Serve with Everyday Green Salad (page 45) and fresh bread.

SERVES

SIX

1 recipe fresh pasta, rolled into sheets (page 70)

2 cups ricotta cheese (store-bought or homemade, page 27)

2 eggs

¼ cup Tuscan Herb infused olive oil

1 recipe Bolognese sauce (page 77)

3 cups grated mozzarella cheese

VEGETARIAN VARIATION

Dice onion and mince the garlic. Heat the olive oil over medium heat and sauté onion and garlic in a large saucepan. Continue to cook until translucent and soft, about 2–3 minutes. Add salt to allow the onions to sweat and continue to cook an additional minute.

Add in the spinach and mushrooms, cooking until the spinach has wilted. Pour in the tomato juice, then gently add the tomatoes, crushing each in your hand before adding to the pan.

Reduce heat and allow the sauce to simmer about 10 minutes. Add in spices, then continue to cook, allowing the sauce to reduce and become very thick.

Assemble the lasagne—with the fresh pasta and cheeses—as directed in original lasagna recipe, replacing the Bolognese sauce with the vegetarian sauce above.

Water bath instructions for thawed-out lasagna
After thawing out frozen lasagna, cooking it in a water bath allows it to heat evenly and prevents the center from staying cold or not completely cooked through; it also ensures the edges won't be crispy or burnt.

Place the lasagna (still in the pan it was frozen and thawed in) in a larger baking dish that allows 1 inch of space around the outside of the smaller pan. Place both in a preheated oven (350°F), and with a liquid measuring cup, pour water into the outer baking dish until it it comes up to within ½ an inch of the top of the lasagna pan.

1 large yellow onion

4 cloves garlic

2 Tbsp Tuscan Herb infused olive oil

1 tsp sea salt

4 cups fresh torn spinach

3 cups diced mushrooms

1 (28 oz) can Roma tomatoes

2 sprigs rosemary

4 sprigs thyme

¼ cup flat-leaf parsley

¼ cup fresh basil leaves

1 (5½ oz) can tomato paste

BAKED CHEESE RAVIOLI

This recipe is dangerously good. During the photo shoot for this book, this was the first dish to disappear. A ravioli press makes homemade ravioli a breeze, although you can't go wrong with a traditional handheld cutting wheel. The cutting is slightly more time-consuming, but equipment set-up time is nil.

——————————

Line a baking tray with parchment paper and sprinkle liberally with flour.

In a small bowl, mix together the ricotta, Parmesan, olive oil, and egg to form a smooth, creamy mixture.

Lay a sheet of pasta over a ravioli mold and gently press on the spaces to make little cups for the filling. The sheet needs to be just over twice as long as the mold. Place 2 tsp of ricotta filling in each cup and then fold the long end of the pasta sheet over top to make the lids. Gently press down on the pasta, then roll a rolling pin over the top to seal and separate them. You may need someone to hold down the far side of the pan when rolling the opposite end so it doesn't flip or jump off the counter. Gently remove the individual ravioli from the mold, dust them with flour, and sit them on the prepared baking tray. Repeat with the remaining pasta and filling.

(If you're using a cutting wheel, place the pasta sheets on a floured countertop. Dot 2 tsp of the ricotta mixture over one half of the pasta sheet at least 1½ inches apart. Fold the bottom half of the sheet over the top half and gently press down around the cheese dollops. Cut out the ravioli with a pizza wheel and ensure the edges are pressed well together. If they aren't sticking well, dampen them with water.)

Bring a saucepan of heavily salted water to a boil over high heat, and then add the ravioli and 1 cup of

SERVES
FOUR
———

¾ cup ricotta cheese (store-bought or homemade, page 27)

¼ cup grated Parmesan cheese

2 Tbsp Tuscan Herb infused olive oil

1 egg

1 recipe fresh pasta, cut into two evenly sized sheets (page 70)

1 recipe Alfredo sauce (page 76)

1 cup grated mozzarella cheese

cold water. Bring the water back to a boil and then immediately remove the ravioli, draining off any excess water.

Preheat the oven to 350°F. Lightly grease a 9- x 13-inch baking dish with a little bit of olive oil.

Spread about ½ cup of the Alfredo sauce over the bottom of the dish, and then place the ravioli on top. Pour over the remaining Alfredo sauce and gently shake or tap the pan to allow it to fill in all the cracks and settle into the dish. Sprinkle the grated mozzarella evenly over top.

Bake for 20 minutes, until the Alfredo sauce is bubbling and the top is golden brown.

Serve immediately with fresh crusty bread or Deep-Dish Focaccia (page 22) and Lemon Grilled Caesar Salad (page 43) for a warm, comforting summer meal. In the unlikely event of leftovers, the ravioli can be stored in an airtight container in the fridge for up to 1 week.

EASY SAUSAGE PENNE with ROSÉ SAUCE

Rosé sauce has to be one of my favorites—not quite Alfredo, not quite tomato, it's rich and creamy and everything delicious. Spicy Italian sausage is best for this, if you like spice, as it complements the creamy sauce beautifully. If you're not big on spice, mild Italian sausage is just fine.

———————

In a large frying pan over medium-high heat, warm a little bit of olive oil and sear the sausages on all sides. Remove from the heat and slice the sausages into 1-inch rounds. Put them back in the pan and brown on all sides. Set aside.

Bring a large saucepan of heavily salted water to a boil over high heat and cook the penne, stirring to avoid sticking, until it's al dente.

In a separate large saucepan over medium heat, mix the Pomodoro sauce with the cream and 2 Tbsp of the olive oil to combine. Bring to a simmer. Add the Italian sausage rounds.

When the pasta is cooked, drain it and toss it with the remaining 2 Tbsp olive oil. Add it to the sauce and cook over medium heat, reducing the sauce slightly and allowing it to fully coat the penne, 2–3 minutes.

Serve the pasta in individual dishes, topped with Parmesan cheese. Leftovers can be stored in an airtight container in the fridge for up to 1 week.

SERVES
TWO

———

3 spicy Italian sausages

1½ cups dried penne

1 cup Pomodoro sauce (page 75)

½ cup whipping (35%) cream

4 Tbsp Tuscan Herb infused olive oil, divided

Grated Parmesan cheese for garnish

CACIO E PEPE

When it comes to late night cravings, I long for this. Simple, easy, and delicious, this pasta is as easy as it gets. Using the best ingredients is key to turning out the best dish, and the Tuscan Herb infused olive oil takes it to a whole new level. Traditionally it calls for bucatini-a spaghetti like pasta that has a tiny hole running through the center—although I use just regular spaghetti. For special occasions use squid ink pasta to liven the dish up even more.

———————————

Bring a large pot of water to a rolling boil, add the pasta and cook until al dente, according to package directions.

While the pasta is cooking, scoop ¼ cup of pasta water from the pot and pour into the bowl with the Parmesan, olive oil, and black pepper. Mix well to form a smooth paste; if needed, add more water a tablespoon at a time to achieve a smooth, creamy consistency. Add salt and pepper to taste.

Drain the pasta and add to the Parmesan mixture, using tongs or two forks. Toss the pasta, fully coating it with the cheese mixture.

Serve with a pinch of chili flakes and an extra grating of Parmesan cheese.

SERVES
FOUR
———
as a side

500g spaghetti or bucatini pasta

2 cups grated Parmesan cheese, plus extra for garnish

¼ cup hot pasta water

2 Tbsp Tuscan Herb Infused olive oil

1 tsp fresh cracked black pepper

Pinch of chili flakes for garnish

Sea salt to taste

MAIN DISHES

CREAMY POLENTA with ROASTED MUSHROOMS and SHAVED PARMESAN

Nothing beats a warm bowl of polenta on a cool evening, especially in the fall when the leaves are changing color and it's starting to get dark earlier. For the mushrooms, use a mix of thinly sliced Portobello, cremini, and button varieties. If you're feeling luxurious, this dish is lovely with chanterelle, lobster, and fresh porcini mushrooms.

SERVES
FOUR

5 cups chicken broth (page 49)

1 cup cornmeal

1½ cups sliced mixed mushrooms

4 garlic cloves

2 sprigs rosemary

¼ cup + 2 Tbsp extra virgin olive oil, divided

1 Tbsp Fig dark balsamic vinegar

¼ cup grated Parmesan cheese

Shaved Parmesan cheese and fresh rosemary for garnish

In a large saucepan, pour the chicken stock over the cornmeal, and then let sit, covered, for up to 2 hours on the kitchen counter, or up to overnight in the fridge.

Preheat the oven to 325°F. Line a baking tray with parchment paper.

Place the mushrooms in a mixing bowl. Crush and roughly chop the garlic, and add it to the mushrooms. Strip the leaves from the sprigs of rosemary, roughly chop them, and add to the mushrooms.

Drizzle in the 2 Tbsp olive oil and the balsamic, tossing to coat the mushrooms, then transfer everything to the prepared baking tray. Bake for 15 minutes. Remove from the oven, turn the mushrooms, and bake for another 15–20 minutes, until the centers are soft and the edges are browned and slightly crisp. You want them to caramelize slightly.

Meanwhile, whisk the cornmeal in the pot and bring to a boil over medium-high heat, whisking constantly to prevent lumps. As soon as bubbles start to pop on the top of the cornmeal, turn down the heat to medium-low. Still using a whisk, stir the cornmeal every few minutes so that no skin or lumps form. It will take about 30 minutes to cook thoroughly. It may appear to be done after 10–15 minutes, but keep stirring and cooking it—the more the cornmeal rehydrates, the creamier the finished product (the polenta) will be. After about 25 minutes of cooking, stir in the remaining ¼ cup olive oil and the ¼ cup Parmesan cheese. Remove from the heat and let sit for a few minutes before serving to allow the polenta to thicken slightly. It should be the consistency of soft scrambled eggs—thick and creamy, not runny or soupy.

To serve, ladle polenta onto serving places and create a small well in the center. Scoop some mushrooms into the well, then top with shaved Parmesan cheese and fresh rosemary. Leftovers can be stored in an airtight container in the fridge for up to 2 days.

YAM GNOCCHI with ROASTED GARLIC GORGONZOLA CREAM SAUCE

The sweetness of the yams, bright flavor of the blue cheese, and tangy sweetness of the garlic combine with a velvety cream sauce to create heaven-on-a-plate, and one of my all-time favorite dishes. Gnocchi can be quite fiddly to fold individually, so I often cheat and just cut them into ½-inch pieces—they taste just as good.

SERVES
TWO

2 small yams, scrubbed
but not peeled

2 Tbsp Tuscan Herb infused olive
oil, plus extra for brushing

2 eggs

½ tsp sea salt

2 cups all-purpose flour

1 cup whipping (35%) cream

1 cup crumbled Gorgonzola
cheese, plus extra for garnish

Preheat the oven to 375°F.

Slice the yams in half lengthwise and brush the cut sides with olive oil. Place them cut side down on a baking tray and roast for 15 minutes, then turn over and bake for an additional 15–20 minutes, until the flesh is soft and starting to pull away from the skin. Remove from the oven and allow to cool completely.

Scrape the flesh of the cooled yams into a mixing bowl. Mash them to form a paste, then add the eggs and salt, beating well to form a smooth creamy mixture. Gently work in the flour, ½ cup at a time, until the mixture is still slightly sticky but pulling away from the sides of the bowl. It should be a very soft dough.

Place the dough on a lightly floured surface and turn it to completely cover with flour. Wrap in plastic wrap and chill in the fridge for at least 1 hour, or up to overnight.

Remove the dough from the fridge and divide it into four evenly sized pieces. On a well-floured surface, roll each section into a 1-inch diameter log. Slice the log into ½-inch pieces, dusting flour over each piece and being careful not to knead in the flour. The more flour you add, the tougher the gnocchi will be. Repeat with the remaining sections of dough and let sit, uncovered, at room temperature until you're ready to eat.

If you have extra time and want to be fancy, you can fork the gnocchi by taking each piece, squishing it a little

by pushing your thumb down on it lengthwise, folding the two outer sides in toward the center, and rolling the back of a fork over top to create those classic gnocchi lines. (Or use a gnocchi board, if you have one.) This is a great option if you're serving the gnocchi in a sauce.

In a small saucepan over medium-low heat, warm the cream to just a simmer and add the Gorgonzola. Allow the cheese to melt slightly. There's no need to stir it.

Meanwhile, bring a large saucepan of water to a boil over high heat. Toss in the full batch of gnocchi and stir to ensure that none stick to each other or the pot. Drain the gnocchi as soon as they start to float. This will only take 2–3 minutes—they cook very quickly!

Place on serving plates and top with cream sauce, plus more Gorgonzola for garnish. These don't reheat very well, so they're best eaten immediately. Believe me, that won't be a problem!

NANA'S BRAISED MEATBALLS

This hands-on recipe will take a bit of time, but it's a great way to spend a rainy day. The results are worth it!

———————

In a large mixing bowl, using your hands, mix together the beef and pork until fully combined.

In a small bowl, thoroughly beat the eggs with the olive oil; add to the meat with the onion and garlic, mixing well. Add the Parmesan, bread crumbs, and herbs. Mix well until it feels like a paste. Form the meat into 2-inch balls, making them as seamless as possible—this will prevent them from breaking apart while cooking. Place them in a clean bowl or on a parchment paper-lined baking tray.

Place a large stockpot over medium heat and pour in the tomato juice. Gently slip in the raw meatballs one at a time, being careful not to splash. All the meatballs should be covered with juice. If some are poking up at the top, that's ok. If some are totally uncovered, add more tomato juice (or chicken stock). Bring the liquid just to a boil and then turn down the heat to low and let cook, uncovered, for 12 hours, stirring every 1–2 hours. The sauce will thicken and the meatballs will swell with the juices. Remove a meatball and cut it open to check that it's cooked all the way through—there should be no pink inside.

Once they're cooked through, and if you're eating them immediately, put them on cooked spaghetti. Or allow them to cool before packing them with their sauce into freezer containers. Allow the meatballs and sauce to thaw in the fridge and then use as if freshly cooked—but cook for an extra 5–10 minutes to ensure that the meatballs are hot all the way through.

SERVES
FOUR–SIX
———
Makes about 3 dozen meatballs

1b extra-lean ground beef

1b lean ground pork

3 eggs

2 Tbsp Tuscan Herb infused olive oil

½ yellow onion, grated

2 cloves garlic, minced

2 cups grated Parmesan cheese

1 cup dried bread crumbs

2 tsp dried parsley

1 tsp dried oregano

½ tsp dried basil

1 (48 oz) can tomato juice

CHICKEN and ARTICHOKE SCALOPPINI

I first learned to make this dish in Italy while staying with my Aunt Grace during artichoke season. If artichokes aren't on hand, make your favorite lemon sauce instead.

SERVES
FOUR

Pat the chicken dry with paper towel and use a mallet to pound each breast to ¼ inch thick.

Place the bread crumbs, flour, parsley, salt, and pepper in a shallow bowl wide enough to hold a chicken breast and stir to combine. Place the eggs, olive oil, and water in a similar bowl and lightly whisk to combine.

Dredge each chicken breast in the egg mixture, carefully place in the bread crumb mixture to coat, and then transfer to a plate. Repeat with each of the chicken breasts, ensuring they're well coated in bread crumbs. Place the chicken in the fridge and discard any leftover bread crumbs and egg.

To prepare the artichokes, pull off the first two outer layers of leaves, exposing some of the yellow flesh of the heart. Cut 2 inches off the top of the heads, almost down to the choke, and trim the end of the stem slightly. Using a Y-peeler, peel the stem to remove the tough outside.

Using a pair of very sharp scissors, cut the tops off each of the leaves, so that you take off the tough tips and leave the edible portions of the leaves.

Quarter the artichokes and brush them with lemon juice to prevent browning. Using a spoon (a grapefruit spoon is ideal for this), scrape out the furry part of the choke, leaving the heart intact. Set aside.

Preheat the oven to 200°F.

Heat a large frying pan over high heat and drizzle in some olive oil. When it's hot, place the chicken breasts in the pan and sear for 2–3 minutes on each side, until brown and crisp. Have a lid close by. Pour in the balsamic

4 boneless, skinless chicken breasts

¾ cup dried bread crumbs

¼ cup all-purpose flour

1 tsp dried parsley

½ tsp sea salt

½ tsp ground black pepper

2 eggs

2 Tbsp extra virgin olive oil, plus some for searing

1 Tbsp water

4 fresh artichokes

2 Tbsp lemon juice

½ cup Sicilian Lemon white balsamic vinegar

½ cup dry white wine

¾ cup chicken stock

½ cup whipping (35%) cream

and the wine, cover the pan immediately, and turn down the heat to medium. The pan will sizzle and steam. Your goal is to catch that steam under the lid and allow the chicken to absorb all the flavor. Turn down the heat to medium-low. Let the cooking liquids simmer and reduce for 3 minutes, then remove the lid and check the chicken to see if it's white all the way through. If there's any pink, place the lid back on the pan for 3–4 more minutes and then check again. Remove the chicken from the pan, place on a plate, and set in the oven to keep warm.

Place the artichokes in the pan with the chicken drippings and add the chicken stock. Cover the pan to steam the artichokes for 10 minutes, then remove the lid and continue to cook, without stirring, allowing the sauce to thicken and reduce to your preferred consistency.

Place the chicken breasts on individual plates. Remove the artichoke hearts from the sauce and arrange them on or around each breast. Moving quickly to avoid anything growing cold, add the whipping cream to the pan and increase the heat to medium-high to allow the sauce to reduce and thicken, 2–3 minutes. Pour the sauce over the chicken and serve immediately.

CIOPPINO

This Italian seafood stew is perfect for cold winter days. It's also extremely versatile, so don't be afraid to experiment with different kinds of fish and shellfish. This is perfect served with the focaccia on page 22 to sop up any extra juices.

In a large stockpot, sauté the onion, garlic, and fennel in the olive oil over medium heat for 5 minutes. Add the thyme, oregano, bay leaf, and salt and continue to cook, stirring, until the onion is lightly browned and the fennel is soft but not brown. Add the wine and cook for 2–3 minutes, to let the wine reduce slightly, then add the tomato paste and cook, stirring, for another minute. Pour in the juice from the canned tomatoes, stir to combine, and then gently crush the tomatoes in your hand before adding them to the pot. Add the stock. Bring to a boil over medium heat, then turn down the heat to medium-low, cover, and simmer for 15–20 minutes.

Stir in the shellfish, then cover and let simmer for 5–6 minutes. Now add the fish and prawns. Simmer for 5–6 more minutes, being careful not to overcook the seafood. Season to taste with salt and pepper, sprinkle with fresh basil, and serve with a hunk of crusty bread to sop up any leftovers! Eat this the day you make it.

SERVES
FOUR

---

1 small red onion, finely chopped

4 garlic cloves, finely chopped

1 fennel bulb, cored and thinly sliced

¼ cup Tuscan Herb infused olive oil

4 sprigs thyme

2 sprigs oregano

1 bay leaf

1 tsp sea salt

1 cup dry white wine

1 (5½ oz) can tomato paste

1 (28 oz) can diced tomatoes

4 cups seafood stock or vegetable stock

3 cups shellfish, shells on (mussels and clams work well)

2 cups cubed firm fish (salmon or halibut work well)

1 cup large prawns

Ground black pepper

½ cup torn basil leaves

EGGPLANT PARMESAN

I've come to love this even more than its chicken counterpart. The crispy outside, soft-centered eggplant rounds are dreamy when smothered in sauce and cheese—although what isn't delicious smothered in sauce and cheese?

SERVES
FOUR

1 large eggplant

2 Tbsp + 1 tsp sea salt

1 cup dried bread crumbs

¼ cup grated Parmesan cheese

1 tsp ground black pepper

2 eggs

4 Tbsp Tuscan Herb infused olive oil, divided

1 cup grated mozzarella cheese, divided

½ cup ricotta cheese (store-bought or homemade, page 27)

2 Tbsp chopped flat-leaf parsley

1 Tbsp chopped basil leaves

2 cups Pomodoro sauce (page 75)

Line a baking tray with paper towels.

Slice the eggplant into ½-inch-thick rounds and place them on the paper towels. Sprinkle each cut side of the eggplant with the sea salt, cover with fresh paper towels, and allow to sit at room temperature for at least 30 minutes or up to 1 hour. This will allow any excess water to drain from the eggplant.

Place the bread crumbs, Parmesan cheese, salt, and pepper in a wide, shallow bowl and mix to combine. Place the eggs and 2 Tbsp of the olive oil in a similar bowl and thoroughly whisk to fully combine.

Preheat the oven to 350°F. Grease a 9- x 13-inch baking dish with the remaining olive oil.

Take a piece of the eggplant and pat it as dry as possible with more paper towels. Use one hand to dunk it in the egg mixture and then use the other to submerge it in the bread crumb mixture, patting the bread crumbs to completely coat it. Gently place the breaded eggplant slice in the prepared baking pan. Repeat with all the eggplant slices, evenly distributing them in the baking pan and being careful not to overcrowd it. (You might need to bake it in batches.)

Bake for 15–20 minutes, until golden brown and crisp.

Meanwhile, mix together ¾ cup of the mozzarella with the ricotta, parsley, and basil in a medium bowl. Set aside.

Keep the oven at 350°F. Lightly grease a 9- x 9-inch baking pan with a drizzle of olive oil.

Spoon about ¼ cup of Pomodoro sauce into the baking pan and spread it evenly across the bottom of the pan. Make an even layer of eggplant slices over the sauce. Dot each slice with about 1 tsp of the mozzarella mixture and top with half of the remaining sauce and another layer of eggplant, topping the eggplant slices with mozzarella. Repeat the layers twice so you have three layers of everything. Top the dish with the reserved ¼ cup of mozzarella cheese and bake for 15–20 minutes, until the cheese is bubbly and all the layers are heated through.

Serve immediately with a side of pasta tossed in Parmesan cheese and an Everyday Green Salad (page 45).

BEEF CACCIATORE

This braised roast makes a lovely winter meal. The balsamic adds the most amazing touch—the Fig dark balsamic adds a touch of rich sweetness, although a Traditional balsamic can be substituted for equally delicious results. You'll need an ovenproof, flame-proof pan for this. (I use a cast iron roasting pan or dish.)

———————————

Rinse the beef with hot water and pat it dry. Season with the rosemary and salt and pepper, and let sit for 5 minutes.

Meanwhile, chop the onion, slice the mushrooms, and crush the garlic cloves with the flat side of a knife, keeping the cloves whole.

Heat the ovenproof, flame-proof pan over high heat and drizzle in the olive oil. Sear the roast on all sides. Don't rush this process—allow it to brown fully and evenly, including the ends. Remove the roast from the pan and turn down the heat to medium.

Place the onion and garlic in the pan and sauté them in the beef drippings (add 1 Tbsp olive oil in the unlikely event of the pan being dry) until just translucent, then add the mushrooms and cook until the mushrooms start to soften, 3–5 minutes.

Pour the juice from the tomatoes into the pan and stir to gently scrape off any bits from the bottom of the pan. Gently crush the tomatoes in your hands before adding them to the onion-mushroom mixture. Continue to sauté the mixture for 3–5 minutes, just until the tomato juices begin to reduce and the sauce starts to thicken.

Preheat the oven to 350°F.

Remove the pan from the heat. Nestle the roast into the mushroom mixture. Pour in the beef stock and the balsamic vinegar and cover tightly with a lid or foil.

SERVES

FOUR–SIX

———

3-4 lb beef rump roast

2 Tbsp chopped fresh rosemary leaves

Sea salt and ground black pepper

1 large yellow onion

2 cups button mushrooms

4 garlic cloves

3 Tbsp extra virgin olive oil

1 (28 oz) can whole plum tomatoes

2 cups beef stock

¾ cup Fig dark balsamic vinegar

Bake until the internal temperature of the roast reaches 160°F, 1½ hours. Let the roast sit for 10–15 minutes before carving. Serve with a spoonful of braised mushrooms on the side.

If you want to cook this while you're out, place the roast in the bowl of a crock pot, cover with the mushroom mixture, and pour in the balsamic and stock as directed. Cover and cook for 6–8 hours on low. Let sit for 15 minutes before carving.

PORCHETTA with WILD FENNEL and ROASTED GARLIC

Even though it's finicky, traditional porchetta is well worth the effort. It's so rewarding when the crackling-laden roast comes out of the oven. It's just as delicious served cold as it is warm. Try serving it with the fennel and blood orange salad (page 41), as only the fennel fronds are needed in this recipe and not the bulb itself.

Pat the pork belly dry using several layers of paper towel.

Lay the pork belly fat-side up on a cutting board and score the fat diagonally with a sharp knife, making x shapes over the surface of the belly. Be careful not to score all the way through—the cuts should be ¼–½ inch deep. Turn the belly over and gently pierce the meat with a sharp knife, being careful again not to poke all the way through. Season the meat side of the belly with salt and pepper. Set aside.

In a small frying pan, dry-toast the fennel seeds for 2–3 minutes, until fragrant and lightly browned. Grind them finely using a mortar and pestle, then add the chili flakes and 2 Tbsp of the olive oil. Mix well to combine. It should have the texture of a loose paste.

Cut 3–4 feet of butcher's twine and place it close to the cutting board.

Spread the olive oil mixture evenly all over the surface of the pork belly. Then place the fennel fronds lengthwise on the surface of the belly. Crush the garlic cloves with the back of a knife, keeping the cloves in one piece, and distribute them evenly among the fennel fronds. Tightly roll up the pork belly like a jelly roll. After the first full turn, tuck in the edge of the pork belly before continuing to roll. Place the rolled belly seam side down. Tie the roll in place with the butcher's twine.

Rub the outside of the rolled pork belly with some fine

SERVES
FOUR

---

2 lb pork belly

1 Tbsp fennel seeds

1 tsp red chili flakes

4 Tbsp extra virgin olive oil, divided

½ cup wild fennel fronds

4 garlic cloves

2 Tbsp sea salt

1 Tbsp cracked black pepper

1 tsp red chili flakes

Fine sea salt

sea salt. Place it on an ovenproof wire rack over a baking tray and refrigerate, uncovered, overnight.

Preheat the oven to 450°F. Line a clean baking tray with parchment paper.

Remove the porchetta from the fridge and place it, still on the wire rack, on the newly prepared baking sheet. Drizzle the remaining 2 Tbsp of olive oil over the top of the porchetta and rub it in thoroughly all over.

Roast at 450°F for 25 minutes to sear the pork belly fat, then turn down the heat to 325°F, without opening the oven door, and cook for an additional 45–50 minutes. Check the internal temperature of the pork—it needs to reach 165°F. Once it's at this internal temperature, set the oven to 450°F and roast for another 15 minutes to brown the crackling. The oven will come to temperature during this 15 minutes.

Remove from the oven and let rest for 10 minutes before slicing.

To tie the roast, place the center 3–4 feet of string (you can always cut off the extra) at the end of the rolled roast (it should be cut side down). Pull the ends up and cross them over the roast. Bring them under the roast again and pull tight to ensure that the end is tightly tied in a round. Slowly work your way up the roast, criss-crossing the string as you go, making at least four passes under and over the roast. When you reach the end, tie a simple knot and wrap the end again to ensure it's extra tight. Tie a double knot and cut the excess string before transferring the roast to the wire baking rack.

SWEETS

RASPBERRY ICE

The ratio of sugar to vinegar to fruit is crucial for getting the perfect consistency. Feel free to experiment with other fruits—just make sure they're frozen to ensure you have enough juice.

————————————

Place the frozen raspberries in a strainer over a large bowl to thaw. Once the berries are fully thawed, use a spoon to squish them against the strainer to extract all the juice without the seeds getting through. You should have about 4 cups of juice.

Pour the juice into a saucepan and bring to a simmer over medium heat. Stir in the sugar and balsamic and mix until the sugar is just melted. Pour into a bowl and place in the fridge, uncovered, to cool, 2 hours to overnight.

Meanwhile, prepare your ice cream maker according to the manufacturer's directions.

Once the raspberry mixture is cool, pour it into the prepared ice cream maker and churn according to the manufacturer's instructions. Transfer it to a tub or 9- x 5-inch loaf pan and freeze, uncovered, for 4–6 hours, until very firm. This will keep, tightly covered, in the freezer for up to 6 months.

Makes 4 cups

6 cups frozen raspberries

1 cup granulated sugar

2 Tbsp Sicilian Lemon white balsamic vinegar

LEMON GELATO

This is super refreshing on a hot summer day. Using the lemon balsamic alongside the zest creates the perfect lemony flavor—tangy and rich, but not overpowering.

In a mixing bowl, whisk together the yolks, sugar, and balsamic until light and frothy. Set aside.

In a large saucepan, heat the milk, cream, and zest just to a simmer over medium-low heat. Do not allow it to come to a boil. Keep it at a simmer while you temper the yolks.

In a medium bowl, begin to whisk the yolks. Ladle 1 cup of the warm milk into the yolks, whisking as you do so to temper the yolks. Once the yolks are warm, whisk them into the saucepan with the rest of the milk and continue to simmer until the mixture easily coats the back of a spoon. Remove from the heat and strain into a bowl. If you want to extract the zest, pour the milk mixture through a few layers of cheesecloth draped in the strainer. If you like the zest, then there's no need to use cheesecloth. You can also add a little extra zest if you like.

Place the bowl in the fridge, uncovered, and allow the gelato base to cool completely, 4–6 hours.

Meanwhile, prepare your ice cream maker according to the manufacturer's directions.

Pour the cold gelato base into the ice cream maker and churn according to the manufacturer's instructions. Transfer to a tub or 9- x 5-inch loaf pan and freeze, uncovered, for an additional 6–8 hours, until fully frozen. Garnish with a dusting of lemon zest and granulated sugar mixed together if desired. This will keep in the freezer, tightly covered, for up to 6 months.

Makes four cups

6 egg yolks

1 cup granulated sugar

2 Tbsp Sicilian Lemon white balsamic vinegar

1½ cups whole milk

¾ cup whipping (35%) cream

Zest of two lemons

Lemon zest and granulated sugar for garnish (optional)

VANILLA BEAN PANNA COTTA
with PURÉED STRAWBERRIES

Don't be fooled by the simple ingredients—this recipe has to be one of the most decadent I make. The vanilla is the shining star, so use the best quality vanilla bean you can find.

In a large saucepan, bring the cream, milk, and honey to a simmer over medium heat.

Place the gelatin in a large mixing bowl and pour the cold water over top. Mix slightly to combine and ensure the gelatin is wet enough to dissolve. Set aside.

Split the vanilla bean and gently scrape the seeds into the saucepan with the cream and milk. Add the vanilla pod and simmer for another 5 minutes.

Remove the vanilla pod from the saucepan, gently scraping any loose seeds back into the cream mixture, then pour the hot cream mixture over the gelatin. Whisk the cream into the gelatin to remove any lumps.

Divide the warm cream mixture evenly between four ½-cup ramekins or six espresso cups and place in the fridge, uncovered, overnight to chill and set, 6–8 hours.

To prepare the sauce, place the strawberries, sugar, and balsamic in a blender and blend until smooth, 10–15 seconds.

To serve, set the ramekins of panna cotta in a shallow bowl of hot tap water for 20–30 seconds, ensuring no water spills into the ramekins. Place a serving plate over the top of each ramekin and flip them over, allowing the panna cotta to turn out onto the plates. Pour some sauce over the panna cotta and serve immediately.

SERVES

FOUR–SIX

2 cups whipping (35%) cream

1 cup whole milk

2 Tbsp honey

1 Tbsp unflavored gelatin

¼ cup cold water

1 vanilla bean

1 cup fresh hulled, whole strawberries

2 Tbsp granulated sugar

2 Tbsp Sicilian Lemon white balsamic vinegar

In a pinch, you can substitute 1 tsp vanilla extract for the vanilla bean, but the final result won't be quite as subtle, complex, or beautiful.

GLAZED BLOOD ORANGE GENETTI

Genetti are moist, cake-like cookies, and they are an absolute necessity at my husband's family Christmas gatherings. They are traditionally made with star anise, but this version is meant for the non-licorice lovers in the family.

———————————

Preheat the oven to 250°F. Line a cookie sheet with parchment paper.

In a stand mixer fitted with the paddle attachment, beat the eggs until light and fluffy, 3–5 minutes. Add the sugar and beat for another 3 minutes. Add the olive oil, beating until fully incorporated, and then gradually add the milk, beating as you add it. After all the milk has been added, beat for 1 more minute to ensure the wet ingredients are filled with air.

With the mixer running on low speed, slowly begin to add the flour then beat in the baking powder and mix for 1 more minute.

Drop tablespoonfuls of batter onto the prepared cookie sheet, leaving at least 1 inch between them. Bake for 10 minutes, until risen and lightly golden on top but not brown. Remove from the cookie sheet and allow to cool completely on a wire rack.

Warm the orange juice a little before whisking it into the icing sugar to make a glaze. Warming it helps prevent lumps. Using a pastry brush, brush the glaze onto the cookies in a thin, even layer. Allow to set completely before enjoying, 2–3 hours. Store in an airtight container at room temperature for up to 1 week.

Makes 30-36 cookies

3 eggs

½ cup granulated sugar

½ cup Blood Orange fused olive oil

½ cup 2% or whole milk

3 cups all-purpose flour

1½ Tbsp baking powder

2 Tbsp orange juice

1 cup icing sugar, sifted

GINGERBREAD BISCOTTI

These warm, rich, spicy cookies are perfect for dunking in coffee.

_____

Line a baking sheet with parchment paper.

In a large bowl, whisk together the sugar and olive oil until light and fluffy. Add the eggs one at a time, beating for 30 seconds after each addition. Add the molasses and beat well. In a separate bowl, whisk together the flour, baking powder, and spices. Slowly begin to add the dry ingredients to the wet to form a stiff but sticky dough.

Turn the dough out onto a sheet of plastic wrap and wrap it completely. Place in the fridge for 30 minutes to chill. Preheat the oven to 350°F.

Unwrap the dough and divide in half. Place one half on a lightly floured surface. Using a rolling pin, roll it into a ¾-inch-thick rectangle (for long biscotti roll it out to 6x2 inches; for shorter biscotti, divide the dough into four and roll each piece out to 3x12 inches). Place on the prepared cookie sheet and repeat with the other half of the dough.

Bake until starting to brown and slightly risen in the center, 20–25 minutes. Remove from the oven and cool on the baking sheet, 10 minutes. Turn down the oven to 250°F.

Place the rectangles on a cutting board and cut them lengthwise into 1-inch-wide. Lay the biscotti on the cookie sheet and bake for 10 minutes, turn them over, and bake for another 10 minutes. Remove from the cookie sheet and allow to cool completely on a wire rack.

Melt your preferred chocolate and dip one end of each biscotti into it. Allow to set on parchment paper. These will keep in an airtight container at room temperature for up to 2 weeks.

Makes about 2 dozen biscotti

¾ cup granulated sugar

½ cup Blood Orange fused olive oil

2 eggs

¼ cup fancy molasses

3 cups all-purpose flour

1 Tbsp baking powder

2 tsp ground ginger

2 tsp ground cinnamon

½ tsp ground or freshly grated nutmeg

½ tsp ground cloves

½–¾ cups melted white or dark chocolate, for coating

ONE-BOWL LEMON LOAF

This cakey loaf is perfect for afternoon tea, and also freezes easily. I love to use a light, fruity extra virgin olive oil like a mild coratina, although the Blood Orange fused olive oil is great for an extra-citrusy punch.

———————————————

Preheat the oven to 350°F. Lightly grease a 9- x 5-inch loaf pan with olive oil.

In a large bowl, beat the eggs until light and fluffy. Add the sugar and beat until smooth. Add the olive oil and beat for 1 minute. Add the lemon juice and ¼ cup of the balsamic. Beat until everything is very well combined.

Sift the flour, baking powder, and baking soda over the wet ingredients. With a spatula, fold the dry ingredients into the wet, creating a thick batter. Be careful not to overmix, but ensure that everything is fully incorporated.

Pour the batter into the prepared loaf pan. Bake for 40–45 minutes, until golden and risen and a toothpick inserted in the center of the loaf comes out clean.

As soon as the cake comes out of the oven, run a knife around the outside of the pan to loosen it, then let it sit for 3–4 minutes before turning it out onto a wire rack to cool completely, 1–2 hours.

While the loaf is cooling, whisk the remaining 2 Tbsp balsamic with the icing sugar to form a thick glaze. If you find some lumps, simply warm the glaze a bit and the lumps will disperse.

Set a baking tray or parchment paper under the wire rack. Drizzle the glaze over the cake and let it sit for 2–3 hours to set. This is best enjoyed the day you make it, but it can be stored in an airtight container at room temperature for 2–3 days.

Makes 1 (9-inch) loaf
(serves 8–10)

2 eggs

¾ cup granulated sugar

½ cup fruity extra virgin olive oil

¼ cup lemon juice
(about 1 large lemon)

¼ cup + 2 Tbsp Sicilian Lemon white balsamic vinegar

2 cups all-purpose flour

1 tsp baking powder

½ tsp baking soda

1 cup icing sugar

TIRAMISÙ FOR TWO

Having a large pan of this dessert around is never a good idea in our house, so it's only made for two, and only on special occasions. This recipe also uses deliciously rich Traditional balsamic vinegar in place of Marsala. This not only enriches the flavor but also makes it alcohol-free.

―――――――――

Have two serving dishes, each large enough to hold two layers of four to five ladyfingers comfortably, ready to use. Trim the ladyfingers to fit the bowls before you begin, if necessary.

Pour the espresso and balsamic into a wide, shallow bowl and give them a quick stir to combine.

In a separate bowl, whip the cream to stiff peaks, adding the sugar just before the cream becomes stiff. Fold in the mascarpone cheese.

To assemble the tiramisù, dip four to five ladyfingers into the espresso-balsamic mixture for a few seconds. You want them wet but not soggy. Place them in one of the serving dishes. Repeat for the other serving dish. Top each set of ladyfingers with one-quarter of the whipped cream mixture and top the cream with ¼ cup of grated chocolate. Repeat the layers in each dish.

Let the desserts sit for 2–3 hours in the fridge, uncovered, for the flavors to develop and for the ladyfingers to fully soften and absorb the espresso. Don't let them sit longer than overnight or they'll go soggy. This is best eaten the day you make it.

SERVES
TWO
―――――

16-20 ladyfingers

¾ cup brewed espresso

¼ cup Traditional balsamic vinegar

1 cup whipping (35%) cream

½ cup granulated sugar

¾ cup mascarpone cheese

1 cup grated dark chocolate

ZABAGLIONE with FRESH BERRIES and PROSECCO

This dessert is and always will be sublime. The bubbles in the Prosecco incorporate even more air into the dish so that once set, it's even lighter and fluffier than other zabaglione recipes. And once the Prosecco is open, you have the ideal excuse to sip on it with your guests while you enjoy dessert. Serve with macerated fresh berries or biscotti, or dolloped over olive oil cake (page 141).

In a glass or ceramic bowl that can easily fit over a saucepan of simmering water, whisk the yolks, Prosecco, and balsamic with the sugar until fully combined and creamy in color, 3–5 minutes.

Divide them evenly between four dishes and sprinkle some balsamic and sugar over top.

Bring a saucepan of water to a simmer, and place the bowl on top, making sure it doesn't touch the water. Watching the heat of the water so that it never heats beyond a simmer, whisk the mixture for 5–6 minutes, until it is thick and has the consistency of soft whipped cream. The whisk marks should be visible and the mixture will start to pull away from the bowl slightly. Remove from the heat and allow to sit for 1 minute before pouring over the berries. This can be served warm or cold. This will keep in an airtight container in the fridge for 1–2 days.

SERVES
FOUR

4 egg yolks

¼ cup Prosecco

1 tsp Sicilian Lemon white balsamic vinegar, plus extra to sprinkle over berries

¼ cup granulated sugar, plus extra to sprinkle over berries

3 cups assorted fresh berries (strawberries, blueberries, and cherries are a favorite combo of mine)

If you don't feel in the mood for berries, I also recommend trying this with freshly sliced peaches.

HONEY and FIG SEMIFREDDO

This almost no-churn ice cream is incredible on a hot summer day. Using the balsamic means you can enjoy this even when figs aren't in season.

SERVES
FOUR

Makes one 9- × 5-inch dessert

4 eggs, separated

2 Tbsp granulated sugar

¼ cup honey, plus extra to serve

2 Tbsp Fig dark balsamic vinegar, plus extra to serve

¾ cup whipping (35%) cream

Line a 9- x 5-inch loaf pan with two pieces of plastic wrap—one lengthwise, one widthwise—ensuring 3–4 inches overlap over the sides to create handles.

Separate the eggs and put the yolks aside. Put the egg whites in a mixing bowl and beat until stiff peaks form. Sprinkle the sugar over top and beat for 1 more minute. Set aside.

Place the yolks in the top of a double boiler, or a mixing bowl that fits over a saucepan of simmering water. Whisk the yolks until they're thick enough to coat the back of a spoon, 3–5 minutes. Continue to whisk as you drizzle in the honey and the balsamic vinegar. Keep whisking until the honey has melted and everything is combined, about 2 minutes. Remove from the heat and allow to cool.

Meanwhile, in a large mixing bowl, whip the cream to stiff peaks. Gently fold the yolk mixture into the whipped cream, then gently fold in the egg whites. Folding them in ensures they don't break down too much, while also allowing the mixture to fully incorporate. Don't worry about lumps.

Pour the mixture into the loaf pan and freeze, uncovered, for 6 hours or overnight, until firm and fully set.

To serve, remove the semifreddo from the loaf pan by pulling up on the plastic wrap handles and inverting it onto a serving plate. Drizzle with honey and balsamic and cut using a warmed knife. This will keep, tightly covered, in the freezer for up to 3 months.

CLASSIC OLIVE OIL BUNDT CAKE

Bundt cakes are not only beautiful but also dense and rich—and using olive oil takes them to a whole new level. This cake is incredibly versatile—I'll fold in fresh raspberries in summer, diced crystalized ginger in fall, cranberries at Christmas or for a winter treat, or just keep it classically delicious on its own. If you want something smaller, halve the recipe and bake it for 45 minutes in a 9-inch round pan.

―――――――――――

Preheat the oven to 350°F. Lightly grease a Bundt pan with some olive oil, and sprinkle in some flour to dust the pan evenly. Set aside.

In a large mixing bowl, whisk together the flour, baking powder, baking soda, and salt.

In a separate bowl, whisk the eggs with the sugar to form a fluffy, creamy-colored mixture. Continue to whisk while you drizzle in the olive oil. Whisk until fully combined. Mixing well after each addition, add one-third of the flour mixture, then 1 cup of milk, half of the remaining flour, the remaining 1 cup milk, and then the remaining flour. Beat until fluffy, creamy, and fully combined.

Pour the batter into the prepared pan, and tap the pan gently on the counter to ensure the batter is level and even and to remove any air pockets.

Bake until the cake has risen and is golden on top, and a toothpick inserted in the center comes out with a few soft crumbs but no batter on it, 1 hour and 15 minutes. Remove the cake from the oven and immediately run a knife around the outside to loosen the edges. Let it sit in the pan on a wire rack for 2–3 minutes, then invert onto a serving plate. Let cool completely before drizzling with a simple glaze of your choice or a dusting of icing sugar.

This can be stored in an airtight container at room temperature for up to 5 days.

Makes one 10-inch Bundt cake

4 cups all-purpose flour

1½ tsp baking powder

½ tsp baking soda

1 tsp sea salt

6 eggs

2 cups granulated sugar

1 cup Blood Orange fused olive oil

2 cups 2% milk

FLOURLESS CHOCOLATE TORTE

Such a dense, rich, and delicious chocolate cake. The Blood Orange fused olive oil adds complexity and uniqueness.

SERVES
SIX

Makes one 8-inch cake

8 oz dark chocolate (I like bittersweet or a minimum 70% cocoa for this)

½ cup Blood Orange fused olive oil

6 eggs

¾ cup granulated sugar, divided

Pinch of sea salt

Cocoa and fresh mint leaves for garnish

Preheat the oven to 325°F. Lightly grease an 8-inch springform pan with a little olive oil. Set aside.

Finely chop the chocolate. Using a double boiler, or heatproof bowl set over a saucepan of simmering water, whisk together the chocolate and olive oil, until the chocolate is melted and the mixture is creamy-smooth. Remove from the heat and set aside.

Separate the eggs, placing the yolks in one bowl and the whites in another. Whisk ½ cup of the sugar and pinch of salt with the yolks until the mixture is fluffy and creamy-colored, about 2 minutes. Whisk as you slowly drizzle in the chocolate mixture, and until fully combined.

Whip the egg whites to soft peaks. Still whipping, slowly sprinkle in the remaining sugar, beating until stiff peaks form. Gently fold the egg whites into the chocolate batter, being careful not to break down the whites. Pour into the prepared pan and smooth the top with the back of a spoon.

Bake until a toothpick inserted in the center comes out with a few crumbs but no batter attached, 35–40 minutes.

Remove the cake from the oven and immediately run a knife around the outside. Let it sit in the pan on a wire rack for 10 minutes then remove the ring from around the outside and cool completely. Serve with a dusting of cocoa and a few mint leaves (or try a dusting of icing sugar and a few fresh raspberries).

This can be stored in an airtight container at room temperature for up to 1 week. For an extra-dense cake, serve chilled and store in the fridge for up to 2 weeks.

AFFOGATO

This simple and elegant dessert is perfect on a balmy summer evening—and you can play with the flavors to give it your personal touch and keep everyone happy. Here I've used vanilla ice cream and espresso with a touch of Traditional balsamic to deepen the flavor, but the possibilities really are endless. Use chocolate ice cream to make a mocha affogato; add some maple syrup to sweeten it; or sub the coffee for strongly brewed chai and sprinkle with ground cardamom for a warmly spiced twist.

SERVES
FOUR

8 scoops vanilla ice cream

4 Tbsp Traditional balsamic vinegar

½ cup brewed espresso

Place four serving dishes in the freezer to chill before serving.

When you're ready to serve, place two scoops of ice cream into each serving dish. (I like to scoop the ice cream into the serving dishes when I put them in the freezer to freeze it extra solid.)

Drizzle each dish with 1 tablespoon of balsamic vinegar and top with 2 Tbsp espresso. Serve immediately.

MENUS

TRADITIONAL

Dinner for 4

Carpaccio (page 17)

Deep-Dish Focaccia (page 22)

Homemade Gremolata
with Bucatini (page 79)

Beef Cacciatore (page 113)

Everyday Green Salad (page 45)

Vanilla Bean Panna Cotta with
Puréed Strawberries (page 127)

CONTEMPORARY

Dinner for 4

Easy Tomato Bruschetta (page 15)

Baguette or crackers

Italian Wedding Soup (page 55)

Lemon Grilled Caesar Salad (page 43)

Lasagna (page 82)

Honey and Fig Semifreddo
(page 139)

VEGETARIAN

Dinner for 4

Easy Marinated Olives
and Mozzarella (page 21)

Crispy Fried Polenta and
Roasted Cherry Tomatoes (page 29)

Baked Cheese Ravioli (page 86)

Panzanella Salad (page 39)

Raspberry Ice (page 123)

One-Bowl Lemon Loaf (page 133)

SUMMER HOLIDAY

Picnic for 6

Tapenade (page 19)

Homemade Ricotta Cheese (page 27)

Two or three fresh baguettes

Shaved Fennel Salad with
Blood Oranges (page 41)

Porchetta with Wild Fennel and Roasted Garlic
(bring it cold and sliced) (page 117)

Glazed Blood Orange Genetti (page 129)

Classic Olive Oil Bundt Cake (page 141)

A thermos of cold brew coffee

METRIC CONVERSIONS CHART

VOLUME	
⅛ tsp	0.5 mL
¼ tsp	1 mL
½ tsp	2.5 mL
¾ tsp	4 mL
1 tsp	5 mL
1½ tsp	7.5 mL
2 tsp	10 mL
1 Tbsp	15 mL
4 tsp	20 mL
2 Tbsp	30 mL
3 Tbsp	45 mL
¼ cup/4 Tbsp	60 mL
5 Tbsp	75 mL
⅓ cup	80 mL
½ cup	125 mL
⅔ cup	160 mL
¾ cup	185 mL
1 cup	250 mL

VOLUME	
1¼ cups	310 mL
1½ cups	375 mL
1¾ cups	435 mL
2 cups/1 pint	500 mL
2¼ cups	560 mL
2½ cups	625 mL
3 cups	750 mL
3½ cups	875 mL
4 cups/1 quart	1 L
4½ cups	1.125 L
5 cups	1.25 L
5½ cups	1.375 L
6 cups	1.5 L
6½ cups	1.625 L
7 cups	1.75 L
8 cups	2 L
12 cups	3 L

VOLUME	
¼ fl oz	7.5 mL
½ fl oz	15 mL
¾ fl oz	22 mL
1 fl oz	30 mL
1½ fl oz	45 mL
2 fl oz	60 mL
3 fl oz	90 mL
4 fl oz	125 mL
5 fl oz	160 mL
6 fl oz	185 mL
8 fl oz	250 mL
24 fl oz	750 mL

WEIGHT	
1 oz	30 g
2 oz	60 g
3 oz	90 g
¼ lb/4 oz	125 g
5 oz	150 g
6 oz	175 g
½ lb/8 oz	250 g
9 oz	270 g
10 oz	300 g
¾ lb/12 oz	375 g
14 oz	400 g
1 lb	500 g
1½ lb	750 g
2 lb	1 kg
2½ lb	1.25 kg
3 lb	1.5 kg
4 lb	1.8 kg
5 lb	2.3 kg
5½ lb	2.5 kg
6 lb	2.7 kg

CAN SIZES	
4 oz	114 mL
14 oz	398 mL
19 oz	540 mL
28 oz	796 mL

LENGTH	
⅛ inch	3 mm
¼ inch	6 mm
⅜ inch	9 mm
½ inch	1.25 cm
¾ inch	2 cm
1 inch	2.5 cm
1½ inches	4 cm
2 inches	5 cm
3 inches	8 cm
4 inches	10 cm
4½ inches	11 cm
5 inches	12 cm
6 inches	15 cm
7 inches	18 cm
8 inches	20 cm
8½ inches	22 cm
9 inches	23 cm
10 inches	25 cm
11 inches	28 cm
12 inches	30 cm

OVEN TEMPERATURE	
40°F	5°C
120°F	49°C
125°F	51°C
130°F	54°C
135°F	57°C
140°F	60°C
145°F	63°C
150°F	66°C
155°F	68°C
160°F	71°C
165°F	74°C
170°F	77°C
180°F	82°C
200°F	95°C
225°F	107°C
250°F	120°C
275°F	140°C
300°F	150°C
325°F	160°C
350°F	180°C
375°F	190°C
400°F	200°C
425°F	220°C
450°F	230°C
475°F	240°C
500°F	260°C

ACKNOWLEDGMENTS

Thank you to all the friends, loved ones, and faithful customers who have inspired these recipes and encouraged me as you've enjoyed them. As my food-nerdiness evolves and my love for olive oil and vinegar deepens, I continue to be amazed at all the wonderful people in my life who lift me up and bring it all together.

Steve, here we go again with a million dirty dishes invading our kitchen! Between the whirlwind of recipe testing, taking pictures, people piling into our small apartment to eat all the leftovers, late-night grocery runs, and ensuring that Cedrik doesn't feel unloved because he spent the day smelling an overactive kitchen, all I can say is that words cannot fully express the depth of gratitude that I feel for you. You put all the pieces together and you make this dream a reality. Thank you for supporting my vision and walking beside me every step of the way.

Danielle, you are the best partner in crime, and these recipes would be nothing without your exceptional talent for making images come alive and jump off the page. Working with you is my favourite. I look forward to our days together and can't wait to see what comes next!

Taryn, thank you for catching our dreams, for falling in love with olive oil and vinegar, and for making the book so beautiful and vivid. If it wasn't for you and your vision, none of this would be happening. You are a rock, and you and the TouchWood team work tirelessly to bring the dream to life.

This book also wouldn't be possible without the incredible Olive the Senses team. You are so capable and patient, and have held down the fort right from the beginning. Thank you for letting me take time away from the daily details to make this book happen. I have deep gratitude for you for loving our customers, sharing my inspiration and passion, and running with all of it. I have learned so much from you. What we create together is the best, and none of this would be possible without you, your taste buds, fridge space, and endless energy. From the late-night cooking adventures to morning check-ins that include five versions of panna cotta, I thank you from the bottom of my heart.

INDEX

EMILY LYCOPOLUS is the owner of Olive the Senses (olivethesenses.com), a luxury olive oil and vinegar tasting room and shop in Victoria, BC, Canada that offers the finest fresh premium olive oils and balsamic vinegars from all over the world.

She is also the founder of This Table Collective (ThisTable.com), an online food community that sources artisanal food products, shares recipes and artisan stories, and supports food-focused charities.

Emily lives in Victoria with her husband, Steve, and their pug, Cedrik. She can most often be found at local markets, in her kitchen creating and testing new recipes, or mingling in her store with her loyal customers.

DANIELLE (DL) ACKEN is a Canadian-born international food photographer who splits her time between London, UK and her farm studio on Canada's beautiful Salt Spring Island. A self-proclaimed compulsive traveler, her photography is inspired by the multitude of palettes and moods found throughout her wanderings. See her work at dlacken.com.

Edited by Lesley Cameron
Designed and illustrated by Tree Abraham
Proofread by Claire Philipson

LIBRARY AND ARCHIVES CANADA CATALOGUING IN PUBLICATION
Lycopolus, Emily, 1985-, author
Italy : recipes for olive oil and vinegar lovers /
Emily Lycopolus ; photographs by D.L. Acken.

Issued in print and electronic formats.
ISBN 978-1-77151-225-1 (hardcover)

1. Cooking (Olive oil). 2. Cooking (Vinegar). 3. Olive oil. 4. Vinegar.
5. Cooking, Italian. 6. Cookbooks. I. Title. II. Title: Recipes for olive oil
& vinegar lovers. III. Title: Recipes for olive oil and vinegar lovers.

TX819.O42L925   2017 641.6'463   C20179003720

We acknowledge the financial support of the Government of Canada through the Canada Book Fund and the province of British Columbia through the Book Publishing Tax Credit.

Canadä

This book was produced using FSC®-certified, acid-free papers, processed chlorine free, and printed with soya-based inks.

PRINTED IN CHINA

21 20 19 18 17   5 4 3 2